lucky

an African student, an American dream,
and a long bike ride

Brooke Marshall

Published in the United States by Atramental Publishing
First Atramental Publishing Edition, 2021
ISBN: 978-0-9863979-2-9 (paperback)
ISBN: 978-0-9863979-3-6 (ebook)

The events and conversations in this book have been set down to the best of the author's ability, although some names and details have been changed to protect the privacy of individuals.

For Emily with the cool last name
and for every other smart gal who apologizes too much and dreams so
big that other people tell you, "You can't do that."
They're wrong. You can do anything.

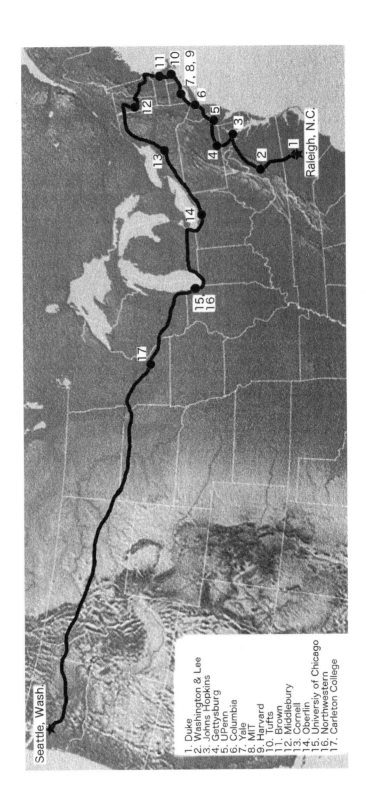

Seattle, Wash.

11
10
7, 8, 9
6
12
5
13
3
Raleigh, N.C.
4
2
1

14

15
16

17

1. Duke
2. Washington & Lee
3. Johns Hopkins
4. Gettysburg
5. UPenn
6. Columbia
7. Yale
8. MIT
9. Harvard
10. Tufts
11. Brown
12. Middlebury
13. Cornell
14. Oberlin
15. Universiy of Chicago
16. Northwestern
17. Carleton College

contents

1

chase your dreams

People are always saying "chase your dreams" and "make your dreams come true." If you're doing well, you're "living the dream." But also, what did your parents tell you when you woke up from a nightmare? "It's just a dream. Dreams aren't real." So... which is it?

The roots of the word "dream" stretch back to the Proto-Germanic draugmas, which means illusion or deception. Chase your deception? Living the illusion?

It's just a word, you might be thinking. But words are powerful. In anthropology, there's this idea called the Sapir-Whorf hypothesis that says words do nothing less than reflect and define the scope of reality. My favorite example of this comes from Chichewa, one of the languages of Malawi. Kuchingamira means "to wait excitedly for a guest to arrive." Isn't that beautiful? It's such a common feeling in their culture — ooh, I can't wait for my guest to hurry up and get here!! —

that they had to invent a word for it. Meanwhile, in English, it's a clunky phrase.

There's no Chichewa word for "bored."

So what does it mean that linguistically, Americans conflate dream with desire? If you ask me, it subconsciously perpetuates this idea that our dreams should be separate from our "real" lives. What's real is tangible: our cars, our houses, our phones. A dream is just something to talk about doing, not to actually do.

But what if you did? What if you pursued your dreams with the same focus you're supposed to reserve for school, career, and relationships?

Why don't you do it and find out?

I can't tell you it's easy. There's a reason they say "chase your dreams" — those fuckers will try to outrun you at every turn. But I can tell you it's possible. If nothing else, my experience is proof of that.

I once saw a video of a pod of killer whales hunting a gray whale and her calf. There was no stealth: The orcas just patiently followed their prey with chilling persistence. Gradually, the calf became too exhausted to swim, and the orcas descended.

You're the orca in this scenario.

I know there are reasons not to chase your dreams — good reasons, personal reasons, legitimate reasons. Put them aside. I want to give you a map.

*

In the summer of 2018, I rode a bike named Lucky from Raleigh to Seattle. I covered 5,085 miles in a little over three months, solo.

We live in a world where women can travel safely alone, but not quite in a world where they all believe it. At the New

Rochelle Diner just outside of New York City, an elderly couple at the next table over bought my lunch.

"You're a brave girl," the woman said.

I gave her a warm, encouraging smile. "You and I both know that a woman can do anything a man can do."

"That's right," she said, straightening and brightening like I'd reminded her. "That's *right*."

The first time I traveled alone was when I was 20. I had a volunteer gig teaching English in Slovakia and Hungary, and I decided to take a couple weeks beforehand to bounce around Western Europe. In the weeks leading up to my trip, I became consumed with dread. A couple of my well-off friends were going on an expensive tour package with group horseback rides and guides to make sure you didn't get murdered. Meanwhile all I could afford were 17-bed dorms in the red-light district. I was doomed.

But shortly after I arrived, I discovered the unexpected benefits of solo travel in the form of 10-cent dinner rolls at a bakery in Berlin.

"10 cents?" I asked incredulously.

"Ja."

Traveling alone means there's no one to question the wisdom of subsisting solely on dinner rolls for two solid days.

For fun, I visited all the free attractions listed in the *Lonely Planet*. To save money, I walked. In an alley near the East Side Gallery, I met a Sudanese refugee named Ouda. We smoked a joint on the banks of the Berlin River, and he told me about fighting in Darfur.

"I saw too many dead bodies," he said. "Too many arms and legs. It was real bullshit."

I thanked him for sharing his story with me, and we split a dinner roll. Later that night in the hostel lounge, these two

German guys shared their beer with me, and I goaded one of them into writing me a love poem.

For the love that she from me took
Her hair was blond, her name was Brooke...

Traveling alone means there's no one to protect you from all the most interesting parts of travel.

Of course, solo travel isn't all love poems and war stories. It's also a lot of, well, alone time. How did I occupy the hours? I played games with myself, of course! Like my perennial favorite, What Am I Grateful For?

Things didn't always go according to plan, but they still worked out. Like when I missed a train and thought I was stranded in Paris, but

> **how to play What Am I Grateful For?**
> **Step 1**: List everything you're grateful for.
> **Step 2**: You win!

then found *1-penny airfare* on a budget airline. Or when I was convinced a payphone had eaten the last of my change, but then my friend's voice materialized on the other end of the line. It was almost spooky. Was Bob Marley right this whole time when he sang, "Everything's gonna be all right"?

Sunset at the basketball court in a small Hungarian town called Téskand. I was playing a pickup game with about 20 of my students, from 4-year-old Marcel to 21-year-old Tsiki. The older kids gently passed the ball to the little ones, who screwed up all their strength to throw the feeblest airballs; we cheered like it was the winning point in the playoff game. Occasionally Nikki would break away to do a graceful layup. The twins, Anett and Monika, were singing their favorite American pop song, Tenacious D's "Fuck Her Gently." I stood there with an idiot grin on my face. I was still taking three Lamictal every morning. The scar on my left wrist was still red.

I imagined the Brooke of eight months before, kneeling on her bloody comforter with a stolen box cutter in her hand and an expression of numb defeat on her face. I imagined I could open a window in front of her eyes, so she could peer through it and into the warm summer light. She sees me, in a brown tank top with ribbons and denim shorts with the purple satin hem, surrounded by laughter and love. I look at her, and with my eyes I say, "Everything's gonna be all right. Everything is exactly where it's supposed to be."

*

Flash forward 15 years or so, and here I am still traveling alone. Once you do it, you realize it can be done. And then you start looking for challenges, like riding a bike across America.

"Have you always wanted to ride a bike across America?" was a question I got sometimes. And the answer is: Honestly, not really. We adults do this thing where we superimpose our current desires onto our past selves. "I've wanted to do this since I was a kid" — as if the only justification for actually living a dream is if you've been waiting a lifetime to do it.

Well, how's this for a confession: I *hated* biking when I was a kid. We lived on a winding dirt road at the top of a hill, so for me, "biking" meant a few terrifying minutes of riding the brakes and trying not to fly over my handlebars, and then pushing my heavy-ass thrift-store Huffy two miles uphill.

Years later in college, I bought a $25 mountain bike to commute to my summer internship. I named him Bikey. His frame was eight inches too short, it took me 40 minutes to go two miles, and I got hit by a car, but god *damn* did I fall in love with biking. It made me feel powerful, graceful, like I was moving at exactly the right speed to appreciate the world around me.

A bike is fine for a broke college kid, but an adult needs a car. And sure enough, by the time I was 25 I had a Honda Civic.

I also had a nice apartment, a stable job, and a long-term boyfriend. All the things that are supposed to make you happy.

I felt like I was in a cage.

So I dumped the boyfriend, quit the job, sold the car, and went to grad school to study cultural anthropology. My family *loved* this decision.

"How do you think you're going to get around without a car?"

"You can't just ride your bike everywhere."

"Have you *really* thought about this?"

Honestly, probably not. But I knew I couldn't afford the car and go to school, and I *knew* I couldn't work that office job anymore. Even if I *had* thought it through, I doubt I would have predicted what happened.

Here's what happened:

It's been 10 years since I've owned a car. In that time, I've hitched rides with friends and strangers and taken the bus. But I've mostly ridden a bike.

I've been sunburned and sweat-soaked and caught in torrential downpours and frozen numb. I've ridden on an empty stomach, on no sleep, after giving blood, and on all manner of substances (not all at the same time). I've hit loose gravel and slick pavement and sand. My chain has fallen off and my brakes have given out. I've flown over the handlebars, skidded on pavement, and toppled over sideways. I've patched flats and replaced frayed brake cables and trued my wheels. I've ridden a beach cruiser in Japan and a mountain bike in Africa and a fat-tire Surly in Antarctica. And, of course, from Raleigh to Seattle.

I've known the feeling of freedom that comes from standing on my pedals and getting up to speed. That liquid sensation when the line between you and the bike blurs, and you're a being of pure grace and motion. On a bike, you tap into an invisible, underlying current. You can read the road, and weave your way confidently among the cars and potholes and pedestrians. You are in and of the world. Athletes call it the zone; Taoists call wu wei; I call it "going to the grocery store."

So no, I didn't think it through. "Think it through" is just another way of saying "talk yourself out of it." But I knew that I had to trust myself enough to live the life I wanted. And after enough adventures, my family stopped questioning whether I could do it and started asking what the next one was gonna be. They recognized that maybe I knew what I was doing after all. And your family will too. Don't worry, I'll never tell em the truth: We're just making it up as we go along.

*

I figured that if I was going to ride a bike across the country, I might as well do it for a cause. And it just so happened that I had a promise to keep.

As a Peace Corps Volunteer, I taught English at a secondary school in Malawi, a sliver of a country wedged between Zambia and Mozambique. It's poor[1], and the education system is screwed up. If I may elaborate:

Malawi's official language of instruction is English, but few of your teachers really understand it. There aren't enough qualified math and science teachers either, so it's entirely possible you're learning math from someone who doesn't understand it, in a language they don't speak.

---

[1] I use the word *poor* and not *developing* because as Dayo Olopade asks in *The Bright Continent*, "developing" toward what? Toward developed, of course — you know, like America. That's a pretty arrogant assumption, isn't it, that Malawi wants to be America? Maybe it just wants to be Malawi with enough food. Look, the issue isn't "development;" it's that most Malawians are broke and don't have a lot of options beyond farming and selling stuff in the market for less than a nickel. So let's call the problem what it is. Then maybe we can solve it.

You have to memorize information by rote for the one exam administered per class per term. Of course, a 50% is a pass, so pretty much everyone moves on to the next grade. As a result, the classrooms are completely overcrowded: 80, 90, 100 of your peers jostling each other for space. You're definitely sharing books — there are only 11 literature books for all the students in Form 3 *and* Form 4. You might also have to share a desk, or if you're really unlucky, a chair. Or you might not have either. Hope you're comfortable sitting on a concrete floor for eight hours!

And of course, this all takes place inside a brick building with a corrugated tin roof and not even so much as a ceiling fan. When it's hot, it's an oven. When it rains, your teacher is inaudible, and you and the other students who bothered to show up are mostly concerned with avoiding the puddles that spread across the floor.

Your day doesn't start with school, by the way: It starts with hard physical labor in the field, or with household chores. Then you have to walk, sometimes miles, to school, trying to keep your uniform clean even when it's muddy or dusty. If you're a girl, this trip is a gauntlet of sexual harassment; no matter who you are, you have chronic malaria, and HIV is a real possibility. And if it's the month before harvest and your family's food supply is dwindling, you're getting by on one meal a day.

High school isn't free, either. Your mom might scrape together the $8 for your school fees by selling tomatoes in the market for 3¢ each, but then your dad might find that money and go out drinking with his buddies. Bummer dude, you don't get to go to school this semester.

All of this leads up to one exam, the MSCE, a standardized test that determines your entire future. It's only administered once, at the end of Form 4. If you fail, you have to go back to Form 3. If you pass, you qualify for college... but you have to compete for limited spots and even more limited scholarships with all the kids from town whose parents could afford to feed them every day.

You could have been the smartest kid in your class, and still end up working in the fields like everybody else.

Is it any wonder the adults in your community are jaded? They tell you to stop wasting your time with school. Girls, get married and start having babies. Boys, hop a truck to South Africa and find work there. As for a college education abroad? It's so alien most people wouldn't even know they *could* dream about it.

But Friday does.

*

I was in my backyard washing dishes when I heard "Odi!" — the Malawian equivalent of ringing the doorbell.

"Lowani!" I called back, and around the corner came Friday and Cameron. I'd only been teaching for a couple weeks, but I knew them immediately. Every Peace Corps teacher has at least one kid who randomly speaks English. I had like six, and these two were the leaders of the pack.

Cameron swaggers, wears a sly grin, and avoids eye contact, so a conversation with him feels like a shady drug deal. Which is amusing, given that we're usually talking about his dreams of higher education.

"Madam, we are proud[2] of you," he said. "We have come here today according to a certain program." He gave a dry chuckle, one that I would eventually recognize as a sign that he was about to ask for something, and glanced toward Friday.

Friday's last name is Ganizani, which translates literally to "please think." It's fitting. He looks like he might be about 10 years old, but he carries himself with the confidence of a bright

---

[2] I think the meaning of "proud" here is closer to "admire," like how you might feel if you saw someone driving a Jaguar.

college student. His hand moves when he talks, like he's weighing something light in his palm, and travels up to stroke his chin while he searches for the right word. He speaks directly, holding my gaze.

"We want to go to America."

This is probably the most common request Peace Corps Volunteers get from their host country nationals, and I believe the correct response is: "Me too, buddy, I can't believe I ever left that sinner's paradise!" Ahh, but I was still young and green, and so I took a minute and genuinely thought of how I could help these two boys out.

"Maybe if you went to university?" I suggested. It seemed like it could work. How hard could it be?

Ludicrously hard, I found out!

But as luck would have it, I heard about the MasterCard Foundation Scholars Program: a $700 million, 10-year initiative to send 15,000 poor African students to an array of top-tier universities in North America, Europe, and Africa. It was exactly what I was looking for. Friday and Cameron were too young to apply, but I helped six talented Form 3 and 4 students submit applications. And wouldn't you know it, two of them got in!

"Well, that was easy!" I said, dusting off my hands.

Ha-ha, just kidding — it was an obscene amount of work. I helped put together more than 30 individual college applications, and then coordinated the passport/visa/travel process for the two students who were accepted. The whole process took 10 months. I remember 14-hour days, frantic bike rides to town to send time-sensitive emails, strategically flirting with immigration officials, agnostic prayers to the universe, and hours, HOURS of sobbing on the floor.

But I also have the memory of Freza's face when he read the email from McGill that began, "We're pleased to inform you..."

It might be the most precious moment in my life.

In Chichewa, the word for promise is kulonjeza. It's beautiful in the way foreign words are beautiful when they take a familiar concept and make it new. I've heard the word "promise" so many times in so many contexts that the syllables have become meaningless. Just a greeting-card platitude. And — here's the Sapir-Whorf hypothesis again — if the word is meaningless, what about the thing it represents?

Kulonjeza though! I liked the "lon" sound — it reminded me of the word "long," as in a promise should last a long time. In fact, Chichewa has a verb tense that means "always." Ndimalonjeza. I liked the sound of that. What if that was the only verb tense I used when I made a promise?

So I made a promise to my Form 2 students — Friday, Cameron, and all the other freakishly talented kids in their class — that if they kept their grades up, I would help them apply to American universities.

I flew home from the Peace Corps not long after that — on my 30th birthday, as a matter of fact. And then I kept on traveling. I walked from Georgia to Maine on the Appalachian Trail. I applied to work as a lunchlady at McMurdo Research Base in Antarctica; when they rejected me, I went into full-on orca mode.

I rearranged my entire life to match the "required experience" section of the job description. I didn't have enough restaurant experience? Fine, then I got a job in a restaurant. I needed "ServSafe Certification"? I spent $15 on the online course. Experience working in cold, remote locations preferred? I found a job in Alaska on coolworks.com and flew there sight-unseen to spend a summer working as a housekeeper in the shadow of Denali. I renewed my passport and got a professional to look over my résumé and sent follow-up emails and hung a map of Antarctica on my wall, and when my mind wandered, I imagined I was washing dishes at McMurdo.

There is power in focused imagination. You're showing the universe how to make it all play out.

The hiring managers at McMurdo, perhaps realizing they weren't going to get rid of me, decided to hire me instead. I went from scrubbing toilets in Alaska to washing dishes at the bottom of the world. And that's where I learned that Friday passed his MSCE with 20 points.

6 is the best you can do, and a 42 or higher is a fail. Friday did the best of everyone in his class, and there were a few kids who did well enough to apply to Malawian university: Samuel, Charles, and Davie. Everybody else got low passes and fails. Cameron was one of them. It's to be expected; he faced a lot of obstacles and distractions. The future isn't as present in Malawi as it is in America.

But a Malawian college education would still be a huge opportunity for the ones who passed. And tuition is cheap enough — maybe $200 a semester — that I reckoned I could raise enough money to pay for at least the first year. Get their foot in the door and figure the rest out later.

Even though I had good intentions, I didn't want to assume I knew what was best for these people, so I reached out and asked if they'd like my help. As you can probably imagine, they were thrilled that their old English teacher had come out of the woodwork and offered to help them pay for college. Friday seemed especially honored that I was making good on my promise to help him chase his dream of an American education.

I felt guilty that I was only helping a handful of people — all boys, all naturally intelligent. What about my female students? What about people with HIV or albinism or disabilities? There are so many people who need so much more help.

But I don't know how to foster gender equality in Malawi. (Or in America, for that matter.) I don't have the resources to address larger social issues like hunger, disease, or disability. I know how to help kids apply to college, though. So I decided to use my knowledge and energy to give a couple people a hand. In turn, they could go on to support their families and hopefully shape their communities.

You can't help everyone, I've learned. But you can do *something*. And something is more than nothing.

*

Unfortunately, MasterCard wasn't doing the Scholars Program anymore. But I had a suspicion that their experiment had changed the paradigm in higher education. Maybe colleges might be more willing to take a chance on a poor kid from the village, might even be able to see that what initially looks like weakness is actually tremendous untapped potential.

With a little research, I put together a list of schools Friday could apply to — schools like Duke, Yale, Harvard, Middlebury, and the University of Chicago. Notice a trend here? We were asking for a tremendous amount of financial aid: four years of tuition, room and board, books, spending money, and airfare from Malawi. Any school he applied to needed to have a lot of money.

Would Friday struggle in an Ivy League classroom? Abso-fucking-lutely. His freshman year would eclipse his previous ideas of what constituted hard work. But I believed he could do it. Imagine how much more he could learn if he ate three meals a day. If he weren't studying by candlelight. If he had the internet and a tutor. If he didn't have to work long hours in the garden. If his tremendous tenacity and work ethic were focused solely on school.

And just imagine what he could contribute.

Imagine the perspective he could provide in a class about international development. Or at the dinner table. Ivy League schools produce international aid workers, businesspeople, journalists, and leaders. Imagine how much fuller their education would be if they viewed poor African students as people, not abstract concepts. Friday could be an ambassador of the village. He could humanize it, represent it —

2
represent the village

Represent the Village! I thought as I woke up.

"Hey Rob," I whispered.

"Yeah?"

"I think I'm gonna call my nonprofit Represent the Village. Do you think that sounds good?"

"That sounds great," he said. "Can I ride my unicycle across the country with Represent the Village?"

"... Still no."

"Worth a shot," he said, and fell back asleep. I crept out of his room, pulling on my big red Canada Goose jacket and squinting in the broad daylight of Antarctica at 5 a.m.

You'd like Rob — everyone does. Imagine an easygoing old Deadhead with a long ponytail, and then reverse-age him back to 31. He can juggle for an hour straight, he's cleithrophobic so he took up caving, he's dropped more acid than anyone I know, and he once unicycled a half-marathon in Antarctica.

So why don't I want him to come along?

Because riding a bike across the country is *my* dream; Rob just doesn't have anything better planned for the summer. And as great as he is, I don't want to date him. The nice thing about seasonal work is you have a built-in excuse to break up, with no hard feelings. But if we spend the next three months together, all day every day? We'd either lapse back into this not-quite-relationship or murder each other in cold blood.

More importantly, I'm on a mission to help my kids. But if Rob came, everyone would be like, "That dude's on a unicycle!"

No. I have to do this alone.

I decided to go to the galley and get some work done on Represent the Village. You'd think a lunchlady would avoid the cafeteria when she's not on the clock, but it's actually peaceful when it's empty. It's a big, two-tiered room with a long wall of windows, so when you're wiping down tables, you can look outside and remind yourself that you're wiping down tables in *Antarctica*. Between meal periods, you can hear the echo of music from the kitchen, the chefs prepping breakfast to Slayer.

No distractions and endless free coffee make it an ideal spot to refine my dream, to fill in some of the details on my map. The first step of any adventure? A to-do list!

to do
- sign up for Warm Showers
- research gear
- finalize list of schools
- figure out Jill's graduation logistics
- contact schools
- create GoFundMe for RTV
- Malawi plane tickets/lodging
- finalize route

Over the course of the next several weeks, that neat sheet of paper would be stained with coffee, crumpled and shoved in my backpack, and scrawled with notes as one by one I crossed off each bullet point.

✗ sign up for Warm Showers

An awkwardly named website that's basically couch surfing for long-distance cyclists.

✗ research gear

I'd never done a bike tour before, but I figured it couldn't be that different from a thru-hike. That's the great thing about living your dreams: The skills from one adventure carry over to the next one. And you meet people who've done the things you want to do — like my friends Tom, John, and Graylan. I picked their brains about gear and routes and general advice, and then crosschecked this information against Reddit posts and Best of the Year lists from outdoor magazines. I may be an adventurer, but I'm still a Capricorn, and Capricorns don't just jump in willy-nilly.

At the same time, as a former member of a 12-step program, I know that control is an illusion. "The Trail provides," we used to say on the AT, and it goes both ways. Some days the Trail provides a cooler full of beer that a Good Samaritan left at a road crossing. Other days, it provides rain and mosquitoes. I learned to accept what the Trail had to give, and be grateful when I got lucky.

Like with my bike, for instance.

How lucky am I that, after budgeting $1,500 for a bike, REI just happened to have touring bikes on clearance for half that? And that there were only two sizes: large and extra-large? How about that I had decided on the extra-large (because so am I), but forgot my wallet in my room, and when I ran back to get it, my wilderness guide roommate just happened to be there and advised me to get the large instead?

"I am so lucky I ran into you!" I told her, raced back to the computer kiosk, and hit Purchase.

The Co-op Cycles ADV 3.1. Hard to believe they made more than just one. Considering all the stars that had to align to bring this bike to me, and considering it was green, I decided I'd call him Lucky.

✗ **finalize list of schools**
✗ **figure out Jill's graduation logistics**

After three years of classes, two years of research, and two long years of writing an actually-fun-to-read dissertation[3], my brilliant younger sister Jill was set to receive her Ph.D. from Cornell in May! She studied the confluence of Japanese pop, classical, and underground electronica, and what it says about global capitalism. Her research involved secret forest raves and DJing underground shows in Tokyo and Osaka. She'd mix Benny Goodman and Fats Waller with disco and '90s pop, while wearing a gold bra, an adult diaper, and a bright orange hunting jacket.

Lest you think I'm the cool one.

Anyway, I was immensely proud of her and wouldn't have missed her graduation for the world, but it definitely threw a wrench in my routing plans. There are three traditional cross-country routes: the Northern, Middle, and Southern Tier. I was leaning north, but if I started in April, I'd be somewhere in Ohio by May. I'd have to figure out how to get back to Ithaca — a notoriously difficult, expensive, and time-consuming journey — and where to keep my bike in the meantime. It would be a gigantic pain in the ass.

Or I could start in May and ride from Maine directly to her graduation... and in the meantime, what, just bum around my mom's house in the burbs of Raleigh for two months?

---

[3] It's called *Liner Notes: Aesthetics of Capitalism and Resistance in Contemporary Japanese Music.*

It was then that the wheels in my head began to turn. What if I just biked from Raleigh to Ithaca? Two months was plenty of time to cover those 1,500 miles, and hey, that way I wouldn't have to buy a plane ticket. *In fact,* I thought as I looked at my list of colleges, *a lot of these places are on the east coast. What if I set up meetings with admissions counselors to tell them about Friday? That would be so legit!*

And just like that, a logistical nightmare turned into an incredibly good idea. The Trail provides.

✗ **contact schools**

To whom it may concern:

My name is Brooke Marshall, and I'm a Returned Peace Corps Education Volunteer. I'm interested in helping a few of my former students apply to universities abroad, including Gettysburg College.

According to my research when I was a Volunteer, Gettysburg offered the possibility of meeting the full demonstrated need for international students. Is this still the case?

Thanks very much for your help,

Brooke Marshall

I read the email over for the 20th time, looking for anything that might embarrass me. And then I took a deep breath and hit Send.

Ostensibly, I was putting out my feelers and gathering information, but this was also a symbolic act. I was setting into motion a chain of events that would determine my whole summer. Would these colleges take me seriously? Or would they think I was a crackpot? *Was* I a crackpot?

Well, if they were going to take me seriously, I needed some sort of web presence for this project. Hence…

✗ **create GoFundMe for RTV**

I set my goal for $2,280. $388 would be enough to cover testing fees for Friday to apply to American universities — $98 for the SAT, $275 for the International English Language Test, and $15 for transport and lodging in the capital city. The remainder would be enough to send three of my students to college in Malawi for a year each. Get their foot in the door, I figured, and we can figure out the rest later. There'd even be enough money to pay for Cameron to repeat Form 3 and 4 so he could retake his exit examinations.

Even though my friends are mostly artists, adventurers, volunteers, and other variations of broke people, within a few minutes of sharing my GoFundMe page, I already had two donations. And not long after, I started getting emails back from admissions counselors.

What the actual fuck? I thought. *People are... taking me seriously?*

✗ Malawi plane tickets/lodging

South African Air is far and away the most comfortable way to travel to Africa, but for those of us on a budget, there's Ethiopian. $900 for a round-trip airfare to Malawi is hard to beat.

I messaged my old coworkers at Chikweo to ask how much the local hostel charged. They were appalled that I would even consider staying in that rat-hole.

"You will stay with me, my sister," Madam Phiri told me. She's a short, round woman, the vice principal of the school, and she takes no shit whatsoever. I always liked her.

"But madam, I want to stay for two weeks," I said.

"No problem," she said.

"How much do you want me to pay you?"

She explained patiently, as if to a child: "You could stay six months, even a year. Here in Malawi, a guest is a blessing. You can just bring me a laptop."

✗ finalize route

See front inset.

My contract at McMurdo complete, I found myself back at my mom's house and refining the finer points of my plan... like, for example, what exactly do you wear when you're riding a bike across the country?

Over beers, Mom's outdoorsy friend Kerry looked me over and said, "I have some biking tops that would fit you perfectly."

Perfectly? I thought, looking in the mirror. The shirt clung to bulges and rolls I didn't know I had. I looked like a tube of cookie dough in the eager clutches of a pothead at 4:21. I felt like an out-of-shape girl trying to undertake a physical challenge beyond her capabilities.

This is the reality of my existence: I can decide to ride my bike across the country — no problem! how do we get this done? — but picking out a tank top to wear to the grocery store takes at least 45 minutes. It's that *mirror*. My arch-enemy[4]. Fixed and wriggling in its paralysis beam, I am helpless in the face of this truth: No matter how carefully I cultivate my inner self, it will always be housed in this crude vessel I had no hand in choosing and that everyone can see but me.

So anyway, that's my thought process on a normal day. Now imagine me trying to pick out the only outfit I will wear for the next three months. I am catatonic. My inner dialogue goes a little something like this:

---

[4] When I was 17 and struggling with body image issues, I decided to go 40 days without looking at my reflection. Around day 20, I forgot what I looked like, and in that void I just assumed I was beautiful. Like Nicole Kidman.

Completely by coincidence, the last day of this experiment was my senior prom. The lady who did my hair was like, "Honey, don't you wanna see how pretty you look?" and I said, "Noooope!" (To paint a complete picture, I also wore a red dress with matching Converse. The fringe of my hair was the color of lime Jell-O, because, of course, that's what I used to dye it.)

At midnight, after 40 days, I peeked in the rearview mirror as I drove home from prom. Damn if it wasn't just like seeing an old friend.

INT. - THE CONTROL PANEL OF MY BRAIN

Two Brooke homunculae stand together in front of the wide windows of my eyes. One of them scowls and stands tall: shoulders back, head high, feet as firmly rooted as a Vermont maple. She is a bitch, and she gets things done. The other has the posture of a fiddlehead fern, crunching in on herself, trying for all the world to just be small. Trembling, sensitive, deeply fearful, she feels everything, every burn and barb and sting, and in her heart she carries my heart.

These are my extremes: the maple and the fiddlehead. My ability to function hinges on their ability to compromise. And they are at an impasse.

> **MAPLE**
> *Let's go.*

> **FIDDLEHEAD**
> ummm i don't like this i look fat.

> **MAPLE**
> Maybe it's because you *are* fat.

> **FIDDLEHEAD**
> ...

> **MAPLE**
> Ugh, sorry I was *mean*. Jesus. Okay, what do you wanna wear?

> **FIDDLEHEAD**
> i dunno...

> **MAPLE**
> Oh, *great* suggestion! You're so *helpful*!

> **FIDDLEHEAD**
> ...that shirt from GCF?

26

INT. - BATHROOM

Brooke stands before the mirror in a black moisture-wicking golf shirt and bike shorts. She has the silhouette of an over-boiled hotdog.

INT. — THE CONTROL PANEL OF MY BRAIN

FIDDLEHEAD

...

MAPLE

Dude, we have to *go*.

FIDDLEHEAD

...

MAPLE

Oh my *god*.

FIDDLEHEAD

maybe like the purple sundress or something?

MAPLE

The purple sundress? You want to wear that purple sundress?

FIDDLEHEAD

i dunno… no, i guess not… you can't ride your bike across the country in a dress…

Here's where Maple realizes she's been too harsh with Fiddlehead. Her scowl softens to a gentle smile, and she presses a few buttons on the control panel. Through the windows of Brooke's eyes, we see that she is leaving the bathroom, going into a bedroom with periwinkle walls and a bed with white blankets. She reaches into a drawer and retrieves the purple sundress: sleeveless, crosshatched with fluorescent yellow and orange triangles.

INT. — THE CONTROL PANEL OF MY BRAIN

Through the window of my eyes, we see a spunky, free-spirited gal in a cute dress in front of the mirror. Here is where Fiddlehead realizes she was being too sensitive. They're just clothes, after all. In the mirror, Brooke smiles. The control panel fades away, and Maple and Fiddlehead with it, and there is just Brooke, who is finally ready to go on her training ride.

Some cyclists wear special shoes that clip into special pedals, but I've never been one of them, and a cross-country trip seemed like a bad time to try something new. I rocked a pair of Chacos instead. The sandals, the dress, and all my mismatched outer layers made me look like an exuberant first-grade art teacher. To tie the whole happy mess together, I threw on an $8 radioactive-yellow vest like construction workers and crossing guards wear. And so, for my entire trip, whenever I passed someone in the same $8 vest, I'd call out, "Sick vest!"

What I loved most about this getup was that I didn't look like every other cyclist. For those who enjoy bikes but find the spandex uniform intimidating, I hoped my outfit would send this message: You can be yourself and ride a bicycle.

How do you train for a long bike ride? Long bike rides. At first I could only do 25 miles or so, and when that became too easy, I did more. Soon I was doing 30 or 40 miles on the bike paths near my mom's house, and one day, a 50-mile ride to meet a guy from Tinder. He lived in a beautiful patch of woods, where he repaired saxophones in a silver Airstream van. After I got off my bike, he suggested we go hiking around his property.

Uh, are you kidding? I just biked 50 miles dude, now buy me a damn pizza! is what I thought.

"Sure, sounds fun!" is what I said.

During the walk, we passed a small cemetery.

"This cemetery is over 200 years old," he said. "They were slave owners." I nodded in a way I hoped seemed wise, racking my brain trying to think of something profound to say. *Who brings a girl to a Confederate cemetery on a first date?* is what I thought.

"Wow," is what I said.

Still, it was way more creative than dinner and a movie.

*

Imagine my surprise when each and every school I emailed took my request seriously. It's like they didn't care that I was an unemployed vagabond! I set rough dates for when we could meet — "I'll probably be in your area the week of April 10th" — and watched as my itinerary started to coalesce.

My GoFundMe campaign was also going well. From people throwing in $5 and $10 and $50 donations, I'd raised more than $500. And Ben — one of those strange modern friendships, someone you've met twice and follow on social media — gave $1,000.

Meanwhile, a very sweet guy I used to date was texting me about how he'd *also* always wanted to do a cross-country bike tour! How weird, we just have so much in common! It would be so meaningful to share the experience with someone, don't you think? In his defense, this didn't exactly come out of left field. Reader, I'm gonna give you the best advice in the world, and you're not going to take it because it's a lesson we all have to learn the hard way, and more than once: *Do NOT sleep with your ex.*

I hated to admit it, but I was tempted to let him come along. I would have felt totally comfortable doing a solo bike tour of Malawi — and not just because it's only 530 miles long and 160 miles wide. The people there have mastered the art of hospitality: Guests are revered, and sharing is compulsory. But as I understood it, the U.S. was at war with itself, deep trenches drawn between red and blue. How would people receive me, a homeless hippy asking for hospitality and begging for money to help a Black Muslim immigrant try to get a free college education in America? Would I be better off with a guy to protect me?

I never ended up getting an answer to this question. I just went ahead and did it on my own.

3

you can do this

Northern Tier riders have a tradition of baptizing their back wheel in the Atlantic Ocean. I imagine they embrace the loved ones who came to see them off, and then, amidst cheering and encouragement, bike into the great unknown. 4,244.6 miles later, the triumphant cyclist dips their front wheel in the Pacific. The bike thus anointed is sacrosanct, a relic of the great American pilgrimage West.

My starting point was my mom's mailbox!

Over breakfast, I'd realized I didn't know how to set the combination for my bike lock. It probably would have been prudent at some point during the last few weeks to, like, practice using all my gear, right?

"I am an idiot," I announced, "and the combination for my lock is 0000."

If I didn't leave immediately, I was going to be late for my first appointment with an admissions counselor. So I jammed my worthless lock into a pannier and biked into the not-so-great known — past a CVS and a McDonald's and among the armada of SUVs driven by angry suburbanites on their morning commutes.

And thus began my great humanitarian bike ride.

*

I got to Duke's campus, and the ornate architecture immediately started to intimidate me. What was I doing? Were they actually going to take me seriously? I put on a song called "Manifesto" by Nahko and Medicine for the People and sang softly along with the last verse:

Don't waste your hate / rather gather and create / Be of service / be a sensible person / use your words / and don't be nervous / You can do this, you've got purpose / Find your medicine and use it.

Isn't it magical when the right music finds you at the right time? Singing that verse became a tradition before every meeting for the rest of the summer. Thanks Nahko!

In the bathroom of the admissions office, I changed into my town dress and winced at my reflection. You've heard of helmet hair, yes? This was more like helmet barf. What can you do but finger-comb it with some water and tell yourself you look great?

"Good morning," I said to the receptionist, surprised at how adult I sounded. "I have an 8:30 appointment with Tabi."

"Brooke, right? I'll let her know you're here."

I leafed through an admissions brochure. Which African countries are represented at Duke? A handful of the rich ones, of course. Does that mean students from poor countries aren't capable of studying at Duke? Do they have nothing to offer Duke's community? Or maybe — just maybe — is it an unfair outcome of an unfair system?

There are no Malawian students at Duke, I thought to myself. *But Friday could change that.*

I ran through my talking points in my head:

- Does Duke have a bridge program[5]? Can you tell me about it?
- How important are SAT and TOEFL/IELTS[6] scores?
- Is it easy to find a tutor? How involved are the faculty advisors? Are there international peer mentors?
- Do you do interviews with foreign applicants?
- Let's talk about his high-school transcripts...[7]
- ...and the potential contributions Friday and other students from the village have to offer Duke.
- How can I make Friday a more competitive candidate?

"Brooke?" I looked up and immediately realized I was silly to be anxious. Tabi had long braids, a big smile, and a funky shawl you just *know* she got in West Africa. She seemed kind. Makes sense if you think about it: International admissions counseling probably isn't a career path that attracts a lot of jerks.

Tabi led me into a room with violet armchairs arranged in rows for a presentation later in the morning.

don'tscrewupdon'tscrewupdon'tscrewup, I thought... and then immediately tripped and dropped all my brochures. Tabi smiled and helped me pick them up.

"I remember you from a few years ago," she said once we were situated. "You helped some students with the MasterCard scholarship, didn't you?"

"That's right. Two of my students were actually accepted."

"Really!"

---

[5] Summer school, basically — a chance to get a taste of the American education system and brush up on fundamentals before the first semester actually starts.

[6] Test of English as a Foreign Language/International English Language Testing Service. Did you know these tests cost more than $200 each? And that they're so difficult that even native English speakers fail them? Not to worry: If you live in the city, you can hire a tutor or enroll in a prep class — for an additional fee, of course.

[7] ... handwritten, water-stained, dirt-smudged report cards.

How perfect: a chance to start off our conversation by bragging about my students!

"Yep! Freza's at McGill University in Montreal. He has a 3.5 GPA and uses English slang I don't even know. And Tawonga got into the African Leadership Academy."

"That's fabulous."

"I know... And now she's getting her bachelor's at Earth University in Costa Rica. She speaks four languages. For a girl from the village, that's huge."

Tabi was nodding and smiling. *Yes*, I thought, *she's on board.*

"Kids from the village have to fight for their education. Even when they're hungry, or tired, or sick, or flat broke, or when people try to tell them they're wasting their time, the ones who believe in education find a way to get it. With that kind of work ethic, just imagine what they could accomplish at an American university."

"I couldn't agree more," Tabi said, grinning and leaning forward with her elbows on her knees.

I left our meeting with a newfound confidence. It seemed this crazy thing I was trying to do maybe wasn't so crazy after all.

And then I went to a barbershop and shaved my head.

It was purely a practical decision. You don't have to worry about helmet hair if you don't have hair. But there's also something inherently symbolic about shaving your head, a powerful letting go as you watch your hair fall away from your scalp and drift to the ground in big tufts. Your face transforms as the shape of your skull emerges. Who is this stranger? You feel naked, vulnerable, ugly, tough, stripped-down, brave, anonymous, pure. Like a monk, you trade in your identity to become the journey.

Of course, if you're a woman, people wonder why you'd shave off your pretty hair[8]. They might think it's something to do with sexual or gender identity. Or maybe you're just crazy!

Let people think what they wanted. I knew who I was: A person who didn't have to worry about helmet hair anymore. And when I eventually arrived in Seattle with a halo of new hair emanating from my scalp, I'd be able to measure my cross-country bike tour in centimeters as well as miles.

First meeting down, helmet hair solved, and now I was really and truly on my bike tour. I took a deep breath and focused on keeping my balance with 60 pounds of gear strapped to the back of my bike. That's the nice thing about exercise: It forces you to breathe and balance.

Overhead, pine trees reached their long arms across the road, creating a tunnel of glowing green and shadow. A sign identified this as Poindexter Road. I'd never been on Poindexter Road before.

The last familiar landmarks were behind me, and life had only one direction: forward. Every rotation of my wheels was bringing me a little closer to my destination. I've heard people say, "I don't know where I'm going with my life." Not me! I knew *exactly* where I was going.

Roxboro, N.C.
2 days • 55 miles

The second day of the adventure is when the reality of what you're doing begins to sink in. There's nothing tying you to your old life; you wake up in uncharted territory and face the fact that you're only going in deeper.

In my case, it was a Warm Showers house. As I packed and got ready to leave, a giddy wave of panic rose up in the back of

---

[8] Well, unless it's body hair, in which case we're expected to obliterate it entirely.

my throat. *This is crazy. What am I doing? I should just go back to Mom's house.* But of course, that wasn't an option. In an unfamiliar situation, you turn your attention to the one place where you have some control: yourself. So I showered, put on warm clothes, and ate. Nourished, my body maintained, I began the long ride north.

I'm riding a bike across the country, I said to myself, as if trying to make myself believe it. I traced narrow paved roads through fields of cornstalks shaved almost as close as my hair, past bare trees and beneath wispy white clouds, through the crisp spring air. I drank it all in with a grin, so happy I could sing.

What is freedom? I thought.

This!!!

... and then I glanced over to see a giant Rottweiler sprinting toward me.

"WAAAAAAAAUGH!"

Did you know Rottweilers can run up to 25 miles per hour? This wasn't some fat apartment city pet; this was a proper country dog, outside on a Thursday morning with no leash or fence to contain him. A thick white bridle of saliva swung from his chops; he easily kept pace with me as I tried to make 260 pounds of bike and gear and gal go as fast as it possibly could.

Finally, he doubled back — probably because he decided I wouldn't taste good — and I shot ahead, letting out a loud, nervous laugh to shake it off.

Whenever I have a close call, I try to extract a lesson from it. Maybe the lesson here was... laugh it off when something scary happens and be grateful that you got out of it in one piece.

Which was just fine and dandy until I was chased by another dog.

And another.

And *another.*

On *six separate occasions* that day, I was chased by dogs. Notice that I didn't say "six dogs." On one of the occasions, there were *four dogs* in hot pursuit. The worst one was a shrimpy little terrier that kept running directly in front of me and looking back wild-eyed as if to say, "AM I DOING THIS RIGHT?"

I concluded that the lesson was: Watch out for dogs.

*

"BRIDGE CLOSED," warned the orange construction signs a mere two miles from where I was planning to camp. But construction signs tend not to apply to bicycles, I thought smugly, and approached the cluster of guys in fluorescent vests.

"Sick vests," I said. "Any way I can walk my bike across?"

The construction workers shared a look, and parted to reveal a small chasm where the road should have been.

I smiled through the heartbreak. "I guess not! Where's the nearest river crossing?"

"About 10 miles that way," said the foreman, jutting his chin back where I came from. As he launched into detailed directions, one of the laborers stepped forward.

"Excuse me, ma'am," he interrupted shyly. "How much does your bike weigh?"

Deaf to my protests, he lifted Lucky onto his shoulder with the gentle grace of a firefighter and made his way across the ravine. I slipped and stumbled behind him with my panniers in hand. The world is full of nice people!

I believed it for a couple miles until it was time to camp for the night and suddenly the world was full of murderers again.

Maybe on paper I project this image of a fearless badass adventure chick. Totally false; I'm afraid of everything. I get past it with equal parts compassion, logic, and just forcing myself to do the damn thing.

Compassion: Hey, it's okay to be afraid. What is it I'm afraid of, exactly?

Bears, attackers, and the dark.

Logic: All right, I'll hang my food in a tree so bears won't get it, and I'll set up my tent where no one can see it so an attacker won't get me. As for the dark, I'll just think about it as... the earth's shadow. Because who's afraid of shadows?

I had my eye on a flat, grassy spot tucked back from the road, but when I got closer, I found a condom wrapper and some empty beer bottles. It felt like a gimme from the universe. Like the first question on a final exam written by a cool teacher, something obvious to get your confidence up.

If there's _____ at potential campsite, you should find a better campsite.

(A) *a box of cuddly puppies*

(B) *a pile of free money*

(C) *a condom wrapper and an empty beer bottle*

(D) *your soul mate*

Further down the road, there was another flat spot near a Water Authority building. No condom wrappers, just deer tracks. Now it was time for step three: **Just forcing myself to do the damn thing.**

I set up my tent, changed into dry clothes, ate dinner, and then, surreally, went to sleep on the side of the road.

*

How do you know you're on an adventure?

When you wake up pleasantly surprised that you haven't been murdered in your sleep.

Breaking camp was like a magic trick, making my stuff disappear. Suddenly the ground was bare, my panniers were packed, and it was like I'd never been there at all. I felt like I'd gotten away with something.

I biked a hungry couple miles to a diner called Kim's Kitchen. That's my mom's name, so I considered it a good sign.

Can I take a minute to talk about how much I love diners? I love a country diner — you might call it a "family restaurant" — with gingham curtains and yard sale knick-knacks. And I love a Jersey diner that's all chrome and red Naugahyde and the menu's 14 pages long. I love when the waitress calls me "sweetie" or "honey" or "love."

It's so fun to see the different interpretations of the theme of "diner." At Kim's Kitchen, for instance, it's powder-blue walls and crooked thrift-store paintings and a fully decorated Christmas tree. Other places might be quirky, or homey, or you're in the back room of a saloon, in a white plastic chair in a gas station, or at a homemade wooden table in what looks like someone's house. And the food is a roll of the dice. Occasionally, you'll get a meal so offensive it's an experience. More often, you'll be pleasantly surprised. And for the most part, whether you're in Montana or Louisiana or Rhode Island, you know exactly what you're going to get.

I always scrutinize the menu, and I always get the same damn thing: veggie omelet with cheddar; white toast, no butter; hashbrowns, not homefries. "Can I have that booth in the corner by the window?" I ask, and then I make myself at *home* there. By the time the first cup of coffee arrives, my art supplies are spread across the table, and I'm scribbling away in my diary or working on a comics[9] project.

It's such a simple thing, to sit in a restaurant. But as a traveler, when every day is different, that consistency takes on a special meaning. The familiar ritual of hospitality served as a reminder that even though most of the details of my daily life were marked by uncertainty, there were still safe, warm places where I could find refuge.

---

[9] I draw angsty diary comics about boys and other things that make me cry.

I always tip 50%, for karmic purposes.

At Kim's Kitchen, the waitress gave me a sheet from her pad and I worked out my route for the day. The snag was Route 29: four lanes of cars hurtling along at 55 mph. When she came back with my veggie omelet, I asked if there was any way to avoid it. She wasn't sure, so naturally she enlisted the help of all the other customers. No fewer than three people came to my table to offer their two cents. We cobbled together an itinerary along nameless dirt roads straight out of my childhood. It took me 11 miles to go eight miles, but I saw a deer, a hawk, a bald eagle, and not a single car.

I ate my lunch on the front steps of a Baptist church while a truck idled in the parking lot. A tall guy in a black leather vest and matching cowboy hat got out. He eyed me skeptically, checked around the church, and finally asked what I was doing.

"I'm riding my bike to Seattle, and this seemed like a nice place to eat my lunch."

Instantly, he dropped his suspicions and said, "*Damn*! Well, don't take no wooden nickels. You know what a wooden nickel is, don't you?"

"No, what?"

"It's BULLSHIT!"

*

The Leesville Dam is a somber concrete fortress spanning the slender throat of a manmade lake. It looks like an abandoned jungle gym for giants, or a steampunk PlayPlace. I had been routed here by, oh, let's call it a certain well-known mapping app. What the app neglected to tell me is that the dam is blocked by a 12-foot-tall gate.

If I could cross here, I'd have 20 miles to go. But if I couldn't, I'd have to backtrack 11 miles just to get to the next river crossing — not to mention the climb back up the steep, winding hill that brought me here.

A light breeze rattled the bare branches of the trees and ruffled the surface of the water. Warning signs, orange as monarch butterflies, clanked against the chain-link fence. But there was a small white sign to the left, a moth among the monarchs, with a few hopeful words: GATE ACCESS CONTACT NUMBER.

Hmm, I thought.

I called the number twice and both times it went to this guy Andy's voicemail. My eyes landed on another sign: the phone number of the American Electric Power headquarters.

It took all my schmoozing skills, but not only did I get Andy's cell phone number, the guy I talked to wished me good luck. Unfortunately, Andy didn't pick up when I called... nor when I called again. Undeterred, I texted him:

hi Andy! my name's brooke, and I'm biking cross-country. my map app routed me to your dam... any way you could open the gate so I could bike across?

I decided to give it five minutes before I gave up. In those five minutes, I:

- contemplated the logistics of jumping the fence
- tried two of my own PINs — one of which is 6969 — in the keypad
- Googled "Leesville Dam gate code" (to my surprise, there were no results)

The time had come. I called Andy's office. No answer. I called his cell. It rang once, twice, three times, four—

"Hello?" asked a gruff voice.

I couldn't contain my excitement. "ARE YOU ANDY??"

"Yes..."

"Andy my man, you are the person I want to talk to. See, I'm trying to bike to Seattle, and I got routed over your lovely dam, but your lovely gate is blocking my way. Is there any way you'd let me cross? Otherwise, I have to bike *11 extra miles*, and I *know* you don't wanna make me bike *11 whole extra miles*. Look Andy, I promise I won't get hurt, and if I do, I double-promise I won't sue, so whaddaya say?"

There was a pause, swollen as a river surging against floodgates.

"Heh-heh, all right, I'll letcha over."

And that's how an adventure goes. One day at a time, just like real life.

---

dear fritz and emily's daughter,

Your parents are so cool! I know you're probably rolling your eyes, but as far as parents go, you could do a lot worse than a couple kind/smart/generous people who genuinely care about you. I could tell they wanted you to meet me, but you were out late with friends, and you slept in the next morning. Zimachitika, as they say in Malawi; Chichewa for c'est la vie.

Anyway, I think your folks thought I'd be a Good Influence. Like, check out this Independent Woman! She's Gone Places and Done Things. She's really Got It Figured Out! A common misconception. Wanna know a secret? I would never be where I am today if it weren't for all my screw-ups!

I've missed opportunities and prioritized fun over responsibility. I've given up when the going got tough and slept with the wrong people and blown a bunch of money on bullshit. Wanna hear one of my favorites? Get Fritz and Emily over here so they can get a load of this:

I was just out of college and found a job as a counselor at a camp for troubled teen girls. The camp was in the woods of central Georgia, so I needed a car. I went to a dealership, 22 years old and alone, and bought the first car I looked at for exactly twice what I had budgeted.

That night, I decided to celebrate... by getting blackout drunk* and sleeping with my roommate! It's usually not a good idea to sleep with your roommate, but it's definitely not a good idea when you already have a boyfriend.

My boyfriend was understandably upset, so I drove to Tallahassee to win him back… and consequently showed up **2 hours late to my first day at my new job**. When asked to explain myself, I burst into tears and quit on the spot so I could move to Tallahassee and try to make it work with the boyfriend. It was justifiable, my behavior, because I was doing it for *love*!

The dealership that had just given me a $10,000 loan didn't see it that way. And that's how I found out the hard way that you can't return a car!

I still sometimes wonder where I would have ended up if I'd worked at that camp. Or if I'd gone to Portland or Busan — a couple other opportunities I gave up in the name of love for this guy. He ended up dumping me after five years because of an argument so stupid it's not even worth recounting.

Years later, when I fell for a handsome med student a month before I was set to deploy to the Peace Corps, I approached my decision with the knowledge that choosing love comes with its own regrets. So I went to Malawi instead, met my remarkable students, and found a new direction for my life.

"Ride a bicycle across the country" and "help kids apply to college" are easier targets to aim for than the chimeras of "career" and "love." But please don't take my word for it. (Well, you can save yourself $10k and take my word on the whole "you can't return a car" thing.) Live your life, mistakes and all. And when you screw up (that's the convenient thing about screwing up, by the way, is that it's *when*, not *if*), pay attention. Learn what you can, pick yourself up, and move on.

I guess what I'm saying is, good luck. May your mistakes be big, and your dreams bigger.

*On GOLDSCHLAGER MILKSHAKES.

"Live righteously and love everyone," was what it said on the tag of my hippie tea. I liked it so much that I stuck it on Lucky's frame with packing tape, so every time I looked down, I'd see that message.

Love everyone.

I want to believe this is possible. If you loved everyone, what would it look like? Would you have to expand your definition of love? What if — gasp! — there's *more than one kind of love*, for friends, partners, family, self, humanity as a whole? Do these different kinds of love share a common root? If so, what is it?

How about acceptance?

Our flaws are our hardest truths, and they give love a place to grow. When you acknowledge and accept someone's imperfections because those imperfections make them who they are, that's love. And if *that's* true, then we should all just accept ourselves and stop trying to be perfect.

(Ha, ha. I say that, but of course I don't believe it. I mean, I want everyone else to love themselves and be happy, but like… I need to lose at *least* 10 pounds before I can start working on self-acceptance.)

Before practicing yoga, it's common to set an intention, something to meditate on. What if my intention was to love everyone I met on this trip? To treat everyone with acceptance and respect and acknowledgement of the light within them, the light we all share? If I extended love to the people I met, it could only make the world a more loving place. And with love, everything's possible. Even, I hoped, a poor kid from Malawi going to college in America.

Washington & Lee, Va.
5 days · 243 miles

A meeting room with neat rows of chairs and "Welcome to Washington & Lee" projected on a screen. In a row by herself, a tall woman with a shaved head, notebook and pen in her lap, sat perfectly straight with a composed smile on her face. She projected the image of a young professional — an offbeat college counselor, maybe. At least that's the image I *hoped* I was projecting. Inside my brain, of course, I was a house sitter trying to put out a kitchen fire with a sink sprayer. *Everyone thinks I'm a creepy weirdo. I have zero credentials and bike grease on my calf. I have NO IDEA what I'm doing.*

I took a breath, kept a smile on my face, and wrote "Washington & Lee" in neat letters in my journal. Sometimes your body is easier to control than your brain.

An admissions officer stepped to the front of the room. After a brief introduction, she gestured toward me. "This is Brooke. She's a Returned Peace Corps Volunteer, and she's helping a former student of hers apply to Washington & Lee. Brooke, one of our tour guides, Cassidy, is interested in applying to the Peace Corps."

Cassidy, standing off to the side, gave me a friendly wave, and I instantly felt a foolish sort of relief. *You're not a creepy weirdo; you're a person with a good heart.* Why is it so hard to be nice to yourself?

Next, the officer went over information about Washington & Lee, and I jotted down notes on stuff I already knew. It felt like what it was: my second day at a job I wasn't sure I was qualified for.

After the session, the parents went off with smiling student tour guides. Cassidy stopped to say hi to me, and I told her, "I would recommend Peace Corps to anyone with a sense of adventure."

And then I had my one-on-one meeting. The counselor was nice, but it felt like where I saw potential, she saw problems.

"Let's talk about their transcripts," I said. "I once had a student who was a devout Christian, but he got an F in Bible

Studies. So I asked him, what happened? And he told me the teacher lost their exams, so everyone just failed by default. That's the culture we're dealing with here."

"Well... at Washington & Lee, we look for applicants who mostly have A's and B's."

This is one of the many hurdles would-be African college students have to clear: Their education system doesn't necessarily reflect their abilities.

On the other end of the spectrum, wealthy American parents can buy grades, standardized test scores, and admission to elite universities. The most recent example comes from 2019, when 50 rich families were charged with using their money to cheat the system. Want to go to UCLA? Get in touch with soccer coach Jorge Salcedo. For $200,000, he'll help two kids get in. The University of Southern California is pricier: $500,000 for two girls who've never rowed before to be accepted on the rowing team.

The ringleader of all this was William Singer, a college admissions consultant — hey, kinda like me! He and the parents agreed on a price, and then he bribed test administrators and proctors to tweak students' SAT scores. Another of his tactics: working with a shady psychologist to falsify medical documents claiming students had disabilities so they could have more time to take the SAT. (Meanwhile, kids from the village who've never even seen a Scantron test get no additional time or assistance.)

But now that William Singer is out of the picture, the college admission process is fully transparent and scrupulous, right? Of course not. He's just the asshole who got caught.

Wanna know what frustrates me most about all this? This whole thing went down the *same year* that I helped Friday apply to American universities. Some of the same schools and everything. My student's honest efforts considered alongside all the lies and fraud and privilege. Like a minnow swimming among sharks.

---

dear cassidy,

Girl, I love your energy, and you would be *perfect* for the Peace Corps! I hope you go for it — it's one of those rare opportunities that can set you up for a responsible career *or* a life of fabulous adventure.

You seemed hesitant about the time commitment. I felt the same way. But then I realized that two years was gonna go by whether I did the Peace Corps or not. So what did I want to look back on? I had no idea what to expect from life in the village, but it didn't take much to predict what two more years in Atlanta would look like:

It's a muggy June evening in 2015, and Brooke is exactly where you'd expect to find her: the patio at El Myr. Pitcher of PBR, pack of Pall Malls, same old conversation with the same old crew. Still broke, still trying to lose 15 pounds, still dating the wrong guys. Something jogs her memory, and she remembers her half-finished Peace Corps application. She thinks, If I had done the Peace Corps, I'd be home by now.

She raises the glass to her lips and takes a long drink.

When I promised my students I'd help them apply to American universities, I tried to be real with them. If they wanted even a *chance*, I told them, they *had* to get A's and B's in school. I also gave them a 400-page SAT study guide and told them to work through it pang'ono pang'ono (little by little).

And of course they didn't. Who could blame them? Has anyone ever actually made it all the way through one of those SAT study guides — let alone one that's in a foreign language, and you have no one to help you understand it?

Why are we still using the SAT anyway? Don't we all know that it only measures a narrow kind of intelligence? And that the best way to study is to learn how the questions are trying to trick you?

As long as I was worrying about things I couldn't change, how about this: Was I changing the social dynamic in Chikweo? How many of my former neighbors thought I was only helping Friday because I loved him best? Would there be jealousy, backlash toward his family? Not to mention I was basically perpetuating the idea that the solution to Malawians' problems isn't to improve Malawi, but to flee to a foreign country.

But you know what? Friday had a dream, and I didn't want to be the one to tell him he couldn't chase it. Let the admissions departments make their decisions based on Friday's ability — I was just introducing a talented student to some reputable schools. The world can be a harsh, unfair place, and obstacles can seem insurmountable. The one thing we can control is our own energy. So why not use it to be a force for kindness and equality?

According to the national conversation of the '90s, I was doomed: a poor kid from a dinky farm-town with a single mother and a deadbeat dad. But I was lucky. There were adults in my life who shared their knowledge with me, directed me to resources, and used their energy to clear a path for me. I wouldn't be who I am today if it weren't for them.

I was determined to help Friday because I believed in him. But I was also doing it for my college counselor Sean and Ms. Scott and Ms. Chaput and Ms. B-C and Mr. Trombley and everybody else who believed in me. For this crazy belief we share: Poor kids deserve to go to college too.

*

Dee's house consisted of a single cozy room, with big windows on three sides. There were construction projects and plant beds scattered across the front yard, the comfortable chaos of a work in progress. The bed took up a good 20% of the room, and her dog Bonnie was nestled among the blankets. Books lined the shelf that ran the length of three of the walls; I got the sense that Dee had actually read them all.

She cut vegetables for dinner, doing it deliberately and patiently, as if she were cutting them for the sake of cutting them and not to eat them later. She was an Appalachian goddess with furry legs, bare feet, and the grace of meadow grass. I felt like I was meeting a long-lost older sister.

Our lives followed a similar trajectory. She used to live in D.C., tried to effect change through politics, got discouraged with the inefficiencies and cronyism of government. So she bought this land and lived in an RV camper for the first year, huddling together with Bonnie to keep warm in the winter. And then she built this house with her partner, Zack.

They're happy, she told me, but added that before her wedding, she took a day to grieve. After all, she was saying goodbye to her life as an independent person.

Here was a love story I could identify with. I've always had a problem with the idea of "he completes me." As if I'm intrinsically incomplete! And here were the kind of roots I felt capable of growing. It was like we spoke the same foreign language, only Dee had a few more years to refine her understanding of it.

And then, of course, the conversation shifted to dogs, specifically the ones who found us. Mine was in Lilongwe, my second posting in the Peace Corps. The dog was a scrawny, sand-colored mutt with deflated teats sagging from her knife-sharp ribcage. When I found her scrounging in my garbage pile for scraps, she gave me a wide berth. But when I left food outside my house, she ate it.

One morning I woke up to a strange noise that I thought was my watchman whimpering in his sleep. The dog had moved her puppies into the little mud-brick kitchen in my yard. I named her Pretty because she wasn't and fed her until her ribs filled in. After a few weeks, she let me pet her; after a few more, she would sleep at my feet while I watched the sunset from my doorway. I'd extended my Peace Corps contract and left Chikweo to work on projects in the capital city, but it wasn't playing out the way I'd expected. I wasn't part of this community, and all the friends I'd served with had returned to America. It was one of the loneliest times of my life. Pretty was my best friend, and like a good friend, she helped me through.

Dee's story started on a New Year's when she was in college. She and her boyfriend were driving to a party when they came across a dog who'd been hit by a car and left on the side of the road with a broken pelvis. They brought her home, and Dee's parents ended up adopting her and naming her Lumpy.

A few years later, both the boyfriend and Lumpy were diagnosed with cancer.

"Lumpy went downhill pretty fast, and we had her put down," Dee said, gazing out the window at the last of the day's dwindling light. "And it took Blake a year and a half, and he ultimately passed away of cancer."

Bonnie watched with wise and worried eyes from her nest amongst the blankets.

"And then I was trying to figure out what to do with my life," Dee sighed. "I had bought this property, and I had some idea that someday I was gonna build a cabin and have an old dog to keep me company, but had no partner, no plan. I was in way over my head."

That New Year's Eve, she was hanging out with a few people and looked out the window to see a skinny, scared, filthy dog in the yard. It took awhile, but they managed to coax her inside… where she immediately made herself at home on the couch. No one came forward to claim her, so Dee named her

Bonnie. She still didn't have a plan, but at least now she had a dog.

And that year, the pieces fell into place. She started developing her property, dragged her RV camper out here and moved in, and met Zack. A year later, New Year's Eve, she was reflecting on how far she had come as she lit off Chinese lanterns in a park with Bonnie and Zack and their friends.

"15 seconds to midnight, people start counting down, and Zack is on one side of the field and starts walking toward me. He gives me a big kiss, and that's New Year's." She paused and smiled. "The coolest New Year's on top of the happiest year I've had in a long time." Her smile faded. "And then I look around and the dog's gone."

Dee was crushed. "This is three New Years where a dog appears or leaves. So the story became Bonnie isn't actually a dog, she's an angel. Shows up on New Year's after a whole bunch of tragedy, ushers in a new year of renewal, and then on the stroke of midnight on New Year's, is like, 'All right, my work here is done, peace out.'"

And then, first thing Monday morning, Dee got a call from the pound saying they found Bonnie. "She came out with this look like, 'They thought I was a dog! They didn't know I was an angel. What the fuck?!'"

I laughed. "So... do you believe in angels?"

"Not really," Dee said. "But I do believe in dogs."

The conversation drifted to my bike tour, and I mentioned my boy Lucky.

"Your bike is male?" she asked.

"Yeah. In my world, bikes are like daemons from *The Golden Compass*. They're the gender you're not."

She made a thoughtful "hmm" sound, and suddenly something clicked into place.

The next day, walking Lucky down a rutted, steep dirt road, I glanced down at her. She was big and strong, quiet and hard working, up for an adventure, but sensible about how to get it done. Why shouldn't she be a lady?

4
you've got purpose

It seems impossible at first, but the newness of an adventure always wears off. The individual moments lose their razor-sharp significance, and you have to actually think about how many days you've been out. It's still an enchanted experience, of course. Like strolling up a lovely hill, admiring every stone and spider web and flower petal, only to be greeted at the top by a vast mountain range stretching off toward the horizon.

At this point, you can finally begin to formulate an answer to that perfectly valid, perfectly unanswerable question: What's it like to ride your bike across the country?

Every day is the same: You ride your bike until you stop. You ride until your butt aches and your shoulders feel like rocks and your hands go numb from the vibrations ringing up through the handlebars. (You have to really like riding a bike if you're going to ride your bike across the country!) You pay attention to your brain and body, recognizing the difference between your body's needs and your brain's complaints. You become an expert strategist when it comes to bathroom breaks. It's such a rare treat, in America today, to really get in touch with your body! And your bike, which by this point is becoming an extension of yourself. There's a music to it — tires whispering over pavement, the busy clicking of spokes, maybe the squeal of a brake, and that liquid churning of the crankset as you pedal… and pedal… and pedal.

At the same time, every day is different: You sleep in a different place every night (but in the same tent), eat at a different diner every day (but always order the same thing), meet different people along the way (but have the same conversation: How far ya goin, how far ya been, are ya doing it for a cause, where's Malawi?)

And that reveals a truth every traveler knows: Differences are usually just misconceptions, superficial variations at best. At our hearts, people are just people. Like the time I found myself sitting around a bonfire in Virginia with…

- A Jordanian surgeon[10] and his mother
- A Saudi Arabian artist
- A travel nurse who spent more than 20 years in a mission hospital in Ethiopia
- An Old Testament scholar
- Two mechanical engineers on their way to a NASCAR race

We were all just people sharing tea, cookies, and conversation.

*

[10] He got a scholarship to NYU; now he does Operation Smile in three different African countries. This in addition to providing a better life for his family, bringing his neighbors together, and hosting touring cyclists in his home. Educate the poor and they will make the world a better place.

Slim Rims, I see you are going to be close by. I'm in Front Royal if you need a place to crash.

thorny!! i saw a sign for front royal today and I thought of you. I'm like 44 miles away; would tonight work for you?

Hell yes it will work.

Thorny was an old acquaintance from the Appalachian Trail. "How'd you get that name?" I asked him when we first met.

"Because I hurt my leg," he said. "I have a thore knee."

This was in a lean-to in the woods of Virginia, just short of mile 1,000 on the Appalachian Trail. Thorny was a section hiker, and he was getting off the trail the next afternoon. Almost shyly, he asked if me and my trail family — Forrest, Sacajawea, Scavenger, and Paul — would like to come spend the night at his house in Front Royal. "I have plenty of extra room, a washer and dryer, and I can make a big meal…"

Thorny is a natural-born dad, the kind of guy who can't help but adopt anyone even remotely close to his daughter's age. I was so excited to see him again! 20 miles after he invited me to stay with him, the day was growing late and the pressure was on. The weather responded in kind, with cold rain and a strong headwind — the first of my trip.

Up to that point, I hadn't believed all the hype about headwind. *It's just wind*, I thought. *You can't even see it, how bad can it be?*

Well… pretty bad, it turns out. A headwind has a soggy, elastic resistance, and biking through it feels like trying to escape from inside a balloon. Strong enough to slow you down, but not so strong that you can say with certainty that it's actually the wind at all. Maybe you're just weak! I felt the prickling of self-doubt, the bubbling of anxiety, and the weight of discouragement — and realized that I was having a hard enough time with the wind and the rain, and that these emotions weren't making it any easier. Time for a game of What Am I Grateful For!

- This terrain. It's mostly flat. It could be hilly!
- The rain, because it could be snow.
- The wind. It's… refreshing!
- My nice warm jacket.
- Lucky. My beautiful bike. She's so strong and she doesn't complain. She just keeps on going.
- My body, for being strong and resilient.
- These drivers, for being so considerate.
- Music, the sun, trees, my family, breath, being alive…!

At this point, I was grinning like an idiot. The headwind, perhaps realizing it was futile to tangle with such a fool, conceded defeat and slunk off to pester some other cyclist. And soon the landscape took on a tinge of familiarity, and I crested the hill to Thorny's sprawling forest home.

There was storytelling, a home-cooked meal, a hot shower, a cold beer, and a fat cat named Denali. I could have stayed up late swapping adventure stories, but like the dad he is, Thorny insisted I get to bed early. As I drifted off to sleep, in my own room under a thick quilt with the comforting patter of cold rain on the roof, I added two more items to my list:

- Having a warm, safe place to sleep.
- The kindness of friends.

*

I got my first flat tire on my way out of Harper's Ferry, West Virginia. Fortunately, I've been biking long enough that fixing a flat is no big deal — a pain in the ass, sure, but nothing me and my trusty tire levers can't handle. I pulled into a driveway and started pawing through my panniers. I found a patch kit, spare spokes, two spare tubes, and a multitool, but my trusty tire levers were nowhere to be found.

Are you kidding me?!

Somehow I managed to wrestle my brand-new, airtight bike tire off the wheel, replace the tube, and get the tire back on… but then I couldn't figure out how to use my bike pump.

Why the fuck didn't I learn how to use this fucking thing before I left?!

I had the thought that if a guy had been with me, he would have observed me flailing away and offered to take over. "I'm *fine*," I would have said curtly. But I'd be self-conscious that he was waiting for me, watching me struggle, judging me. I'd fumble more. My embarrassment would turn to resentment and eventually defeat. I'd hand him my tire and go for a tearful walk and come back to a working bike. The damsel in distress rescued by a knight in shining armor.

But that wasn't an option, so I just flailed away at it and tried to make it work. Magically, I got my tire maybe 55% inflated and set out with the idea that I could get to a gas station and use their air pump. I made it about a mile before I realized I was probably going to screw up my tire if I kept going like this. *I'll just push Lucky to that flat spot and try again. I have a master's degree, by god, I'm gonna figure out how to use this tool.*

Just then, a car pulled up beside me. In all my years of biking, no one's ever pulled over while I was walking my bike up a hill. But today, this guy did. Asked if I needed a hand, figured out how to use my pump, got my tire back up to 100%, then left without even giving me his name.

I resent being rescued by a knight in shining armor. A guardian angel, on the other hand, is okay.

That night, I stayed with Chuck and Di. They met through the world of model trains. Di is a strong, smart, sharp-tongued woman who has chosen a man who will stand by her as she blazes her fiery path into the cosmos. Chuck cannot believe his luck, because he landed the gal who's into model trains.

They have no children, just two cats and the most elaborate model train setup I've ever seen. It sprawls across their entire basement: a network of tracks winding among popsicle-stick railroad towns and papier-mâché mountains dotted with deciduous trees in perpetual fall foliage. Some of the little workers assiduously wrench on engines and repair tracks; other little workers hold up signs demanding better wages. An entire world of their own creation, frozen in a moment, until the flip of a switch sends the train skating along the rails, transforming the scene like a smile transforms the face of the one you love.

"It's a work in progress," Chuck says shyly.

Chuck and Di are cyclists — *tandem* cyclists, to be exact. As a gal who rebuffed not one but two people who wanted to join me on my tour, the idea of crossing America on a bicycle built for two sends a shudder down my spine. But that's the beautiful thing about love: You can practice it any way you like.

Baltimore, Md.
11 days · 498 miles

Robyn's one of those people who unapologetically takes up the space she's in. She expresses herself with the graceful authority of a college professor, but her voice always dances on the edge of a laugh, and at every opportunity she will stoop to snatch up a low-hanging pun. Hers is the kind of confidence I can relate to: at once innocent and hard-won.

Would it surprise you to learn that she comes from a family of actual circus folk? Or that she's a devout improv performer? How about that she sometimes works on a pirate ship, but that her day job is social media manager for Mr. Trash Wheel?

"What is Mr. Trash Wheel?"

"You mean *who* is Mr. Trash Wheel," she laughs.

The answer could be fantastically boring: a trash interceptor, a solar-powered machine that collects litter out of the Jones Falls River in Baltimore. It's shaped like a giant pistachio, with two waterwheels on either side. The kind of thing environmentalists might get really excited about but that could fly under the radar for everyone else. Until a genius put googly eyes on it, and the whole game changed.

"How do we get people to care? Social media, using humor, creating a weird persona."

"He has a persona? What's it like?"

After a thoughtful pause, she says, "If you took a Venn diagram and put *Star Wars*, Oscar the Grouch, and googly eyes, somewhere in the center is Mr. Trash Wheel's wheelhouse... no pun intended. He's funny, quirky, he can be very sarcastic, but he's very optimistic. And I think that's really important. Mr. Trash Wheel is fundamentally a being that believes in the power of humans."

He has more than 20,000 followers on Facebook, and it's easy to see why. He's that funny friend who uses their feed to share upbeat and thought-provoking information. He'll post links to environmental news stories, sure, but not the apocalyptic ones — the ones about small changes that have a big impact.

"If I had tear ducts, my googly eyes would be watering right now," he wrote about a potential plastic bag ban. "I am so proud of the humans who are working to make this ban possible."

But he'll also link to, say, an article titled "Bizarre crab with googly eyes dubbed 'platypus of the crab world.'"

"I know as a Marylander this is a sacrilege to say," Mr. Trash Wheel wrote, "but this is my new favorite crab."

"I think people want to connect to *people*," Robyn explains. "So we built a full persona of someone who deeply, deeply cares about the ocean and trash, but cares about other things as well."

To that end, there's fan art and good ol-fashioned memes. There are photo albums of events like his birthday party or the induction ceremony for his secret society — yes, really! — called the Order of the Wheel. He has an ongoing romance with Professor Trash Wheel, another of the family of four trash interceptors in Baltimore.

I would be remiss if I didn't mention what the Trash Wheel family has cleaned up: "1,561 TONS of trash," according to mrtrashwheel.com, including "755,558 plastic bags, 12,109,248 cigarette butts, 1,287,972 foam containers, 1,256,914 water battles, 5,114 sports balls, a keg, a guitar, and a ball python."

"That's such an inspiring strategy," I say. "You're taking this issue that might be scary or divisive, and you're making it fun."

"That's a big part of our DNA as an organization, is we're constantly figuring out how we create something that's a unique and fun experience that engages people. The issue at hand is big, and it is scary and it is dire, but that being said, there's amazing things we can do when we come together."

And then she explains why it's important to stop trash while it's still in the river.

"Once trash gets into the ocean, it's almost impossible for us to collect it. One, it'll break down into really small pieces that animals can eat or that get lost, and two the ocean is a huge place, and the idea of having to comb through the ocean for anything is a pretty insurmountable task."

"So you stop the problem at its source."

"Well, not exactly... Oftentimes when we talk about trash, we're talking about littering, and yes, that is an issue, but the main issue is that as a society we create too much trash."

"Ohh my god, I totally agree. Why is Styrofoam still a thing? And water bottles? And single-use plastic bags?"

She nods. "A plastic bag lasts longer on the planet than any work of literature humankind has ever created. So why do we treat it like it's disposable?"

It was like Robin had gently reached inside my brain and flipped on a light switch. If plastic lasts forever... then why do we act like it's disposable? Plastic is the *opposite* of disposable!

Without hope, people won't act. And nothing kills hope quite like fear or discouragement or complacency. But here's this gal who took a scary, contentious issue and turned it into a cool, silly party. Here's a person using her gifts —humor, compassion, creativity — to inspire a city.

That, ladies and gentlemen, is how imagination can change the world!

---

diner break: papermoon diner (baltimore, md.)

This would be the perfect place to take your new boyfriend the morning after the first time you spend the night together.

By the time I got to Johns Hopkins, I was really getting the hang of these meetings. I would arrive on campus a disheveled vagrant, duck into a bathroom stall, and emerge a polished college counselor. Just like a superhero! I wasn't getting any information from these meetings that I couldn't figure out by perusing the school's website, but at the same time, I was getting a sense of how much of a chance Friday actually had. Rather than just reading a bunch of admissions statistics, I got to have a fun conversation about an obscure topic I'm passionate about.

And in the case of Johns Hopkins, it was two obscure topics: The counselor I spoke with had done her own cross-country tour in 2014! After geeking out about Brooks saddles and bonding over butt pain, we got down to brass tacks.

"What we look for from students from a disadvantaged background like Friday's is: Are they teaching themselves?"

It's a valid question, but it's also an extremely tall order. It's what I call the William Kamkwamba factor.

William Kamkwamba was a teenager from the village of Wimbe in central Malawi whose family was too broke to pay his school fees. So he did something extraordinary: Went to the library, found a book about energy, and built a windmill out of bicycle parts, trees, and scrap to provide electricity to his family's house. He was given a scholarship to the African Leadership Academy and then to Dartmouth.

This is obviously a brilliant mind that deserves a world-class education. But there's a counterargument that if international universities only accept William Kamkwamba-caliber students, it creates the expectation that Africans have to be superheroes in order to qualify for American universities. "William Kamkwamba built a windmill. Why didn't Friday Ganizani build a windmill?"

To which I'd respond... did *you* build a windmill in high school?

I got out of the meeting at 4:45 and my stomach sank: I was heading right out into the belly of the beast. Rush hour in a city of 619,000 people.

Every car passed me too close and too fast. The crosswind threw me off balance, the shoulder was crumbling, *my* shoulders were up around my ears, and my energy was flagging.

Some entitled asshole driver on their fucking cell phone is gonna hit me, I thought. Just then, a truck passed me, giving maybe 10 inches of leeway. "FUCK YOU!" I snarled.

And then I had a thought: I was only focusing on the negative. *Okay,* I told myself. *You're only looking for bad drivers, and you're finding them all. Why don't you start looking for good ones instead?*

At first it was exaggerated. Every single car that gave me a proper berth, I thought, *Such courtesy! Wow! Baltimore drivers are the most considerate drivers in America!*

And then, to my absolute shock and delight, it started working. Most of the drivers actually *were* being respectful. I laughed out loud. Was some universal force rewarding my positive energy? Or was I just a silly monkey who'd played a mental trick on herself? Either way, I felt more confident, and we can all agree a confident cyclist is safer than a timid one.

Eventually I made my way out of the city and into Reiserstown, where I'd called up the local fire department and secured a place out back to pitch my tent. So imagine my surprise when I got there and the chief led me up to a dorm room with a sign on the door that said Ladie's Room.

"It's for female firefighters on duty, but we only have one and she's not on tonight," explained the chief. "I know you asked to camp out back, but we figured you could just have the place to yourself. Showers are across the hall."

This is what I love about the adventure life. When was the last time you were pleasantly surprised you got to sleep in a bed?

*

When you live on the side of the road, you see all the shit people throw out of their cars. There are water bottles, soda bottles, piss bottles, empty cigarette packs, wadded-up napkins, plastic bags, tampon applicators, splintered plastic cups, pulverized Styrofoam, a hundred billion cigarette butts, beer cans, plastic liquor bottles, and wrappers for every kind of processed food imaginable. The unofficial sponsor of roadside litter is indisputably fast food restaurants. A greasy McDonald's bag full of trash on the side of the road is a pretty accurate advertisement for McDonald's if you ask me.

Sometimes there were mysteries: a single shoe, a vacuum cleaner, a white teddy bear with a red bow tie.

And then, of course, there was the roadkill. Nothing reminds you of the fragility of life, as you pedal your bicycle while two-ton death machines shoot past you at 45 miles per hour, quite like the corpses of those who weren't so lucky.

The Cherokee would pray for forgiveness after killing an animal. Deer were a staple of their diet, and every part of the animal was a resource: hides for clothing and drumheads, bones for weapons, hooves for glue. Today, we leave them on the side of the road to decay.

I saw a fawn that looked like it was sleeping. It must have been hit by one of the cars that had just passed me. Another time I heard a far-off buzz like radio static and smelled something like shit and garbage water and rotten food. As I got closer, the picture came into focus: a fog of flies settled over the bloated, putrid corpse of a deer. I retched and tried to hold my breath as I passed. Have you ever tried to hold your breath while pedaling a 70-pound touring bike?

There was a completely desiccated deer, leather stretched tight over bared teeth. And the one that had been cleaved clean in two. I saw the back half first; the front was easily 100 feet down the road. Her eyes were open.

There were raccoons and possums that died snarling, and frogs flat as chewing gum, and turkey vultures gathered around the rotting corpse of a cat; they floated indignantly into the air at my approach. I saw something pulverized beyond recognition, like vomit splattered across the road.

I saw fretful sparrow hopping around the motionless body of its partner, urgently chirping as if to say, "Wake up, please, oh please wake up."

The saddest to me were turtles, their shells shattered like ceramic bowls of stew dropped on a stone floor. *It's not fair*, I thought, glaring at a car that passed me with barely two feet of clearance. *They can't help that they're small and slow.*

Gettysburg, Penn.
12 days · 580 miles

If I've just met someone and think they might be cool, I like to hit em with a one-two punch. I smile kindly, look them square in the eye, and ask with complete sincerity:

"When's the last time you pooped your pants?"

Look, pretending to be cool is exhausting. It's way more fun to get real and talk about poopin' your pants. It's a great humbling unifier. Also the stories are always interesting, involving either:

a) travel

b) drug/alcohol use

c) horrifying gastrointestinal distress

d) all the above.

The shields are down and the person is comfortable — time for the second question: "What are you afraid of?"

It trips me out knowing that people act differently around different people. Without some uniformity to your actions, how can I tell who you are? Are some of the ways you perform your personality more authentic than others? And if so, how authentic is the version you show me? I can't stand fake people... and of course I'm terrified that I'm one of them. Because there are a million different variations of how I perform "Brooke." In Malawi, I was a lovable goof named Masho (which is, of course, the Malawian pronunciation of my last name); on the Appalachian Trail, I was an artsy nerd named Slim Rims. My family knows me as quiet, frumpy, and a little sullen, but everyone at McMurdo knows me as "that girl who's always wearing a dress and smiling." So... which one is it?

I suppose the answer is, "Do I contradict myself? Very well, then I contradict myself. I am large; I contain multitudes." Socially we are reflections of our environment; biologically, our cells are in a perpetual state of shedding and regeneration. The only immutability is change. A brook may not be the same from one moment to the next, but the current is predictable enough.

All that said, the least authentic thing I can think of is the stilted dance of "professionalism." It's just a bunch of made-up rules! Little kids in neckties, monkeys pretending to be robots, damming the brook. Believe it or not, When's-the-Last-Time-You-Pooped-Your-Pants Girl isn't super-great at pretending to be professional.

But I was doing my best at Gettysburg. I had my town dress on, writing in my notebook in my best handwriting, deftly using the parlance of international admissions... and the counselor was deflecting me at every turn with responses that could have come right off a website. All buzzwords and fluff and nothing of substance, until the moment when I understood what she was actually saying was, "I'm so sorry, but we don't have enough money for what you're asking."

We stopped and looked at each other. We both knew this meeting was going nowhere. But it was 4:10 on a Friday, and she wasn't going to get anything else done for the rest of the day, so she asked me about my tour. We both visibly relaxed, and ended up chit-chatting for a bit while she ran out the clock. I didn't ask her when she'd last pooped her pants, but for a moment, at least, the kids took off their neckties, the monkeys stopped beeping, and the brook flowed freely.

*

That night, I stayed with a woman named Charna. She's soft-spoken and small, as imposing as a wintertime shrub.

But talk to her. You'll find out she left behind a career as a biologist to be a wildland firefighter, and spent years jumping out of helicopters with men young enough to be her sons. She had to give that up when she turned 45, of course, but she couldn't bring herself to go sit still in a laboratory, so now she works as a handywoman and goes on long bike and kayak trips on the weekends.

What could be tougher than bare, living branches in the cold winter wind?

*

I hate technology, and I'm convinced robots are taking over the world, but the dearth of paper maps designed for touring cyclists meant I was stuck with that certain well-known mapping app that led me to the Leesville Dam. I came to personify him, and even gave him a name: Mapsy. If I was the captain of this voyage and Lucky was my trusty ship, Mapsy was the bumbling, flustered navigator.

Routing me across a restricted dam was just the first of Mapsy's many well-meaning but blundering suggestions. Sometimes he'd try to get cute and route me through a park — to save me riding .25 miles on a city street or some nonsense. But with no road signs to direct me, he'd get vague.

"Turn left," he'd say.

I'd look left. There would be no left turn, just a thick grove of trees. *Does Mapsy want me to bushwhack?*

"Turn left," Mapsy would insist.

That turn up ahead? Or the one like 10 feet beyond it? Or do you want me to bear left at the fork just beyond that? This park is a nothing but a network of unnamed left-hand turns, Mapsy, can you please *be more specific?*

I would inevitably choose the wrong one. Mapsy would get flustered and crash; I would never notice. Miles later, I would think, *Huh, haven't heard from Mapsy in awhile.* Inevitably, this mistake would add another couple miles to my day.

And another thing! Mapsy, why must you always wait until the best part of my favorite song to tell me when to turn? (Or worse yet, to "Continue straight." THANK YOU SO MUCH, MAPSY.)

"In 1000 feet, turn left onto bi-sike-le-pa Route S."

What is bi-sike-le-pa? I thought. Maybe like how some states call their roads "pikes," Pennsylvania calls them bi-sike-le-pa?

"In 500 feet, turn left onto bi-sike-le-pa Route S."

Dude, Mapsy, I fucking get it, I'm gonna turn left on the one left-hand turn on this road with no other intersections. Now shut up, it's the best part of my favorite song.

"Turn left onto bi-sike-le-pa Route S," Mapsy interjected.

GOD DAMMIT MAPSY, WHAT THE FUCK EVEN IS BI-SIKE-LE-PA?!?

And then I saw the road sign and groaned. "Mapsy, it's pronounced *Bicycle PA!*"

We got some time before these robots take over the world.

*

The ballet of the 'burbs. First come the runners, with their earbuds and bright shoes, diligently getting their workout in before the workday begins. As the morning wears on, they weave and juke to avoid the waves of pajama-clad dog-walkers, usually staring at their phones while their dogs strain at their leashes. Their numbers thin, and they change costumes. Now they play the role of professionals: collared shirts and laptop bags, coffee balanced on the car roof, some of them already barking into those ubiquitous cellphones. And finally, the stressed-out parents appear, shoving their protesting children into SUVs.

Biking life, I was learning, meant there was usually a windshield between me and the people I met. But for these magic few hours, at least, I got a glimpse of the humans behind all the glass and steel.

This place feels like you're sitting in your country aunt's kitchen, and the cottage cheese and fruit plate was the cutest thing I've ever eaten.

Philadelphia, Penn.
14 days • 720 miles

That morning, I crawled out of a tent outside a volunteer fire department in Amish country. That evening, I was sitting at a patio in a trendy Philadelphia neighborhood eating gluten-free pasta salad with a group of young professionals. Between those two points, I waved at an Amish couple on a tandem bike wearing the same reflective vests as me, ate breakfast at a '50s-style diner where the owners led the patrons in the pledge of allegiance, and got caught in traffic because of a regatta.

This is the gleeful unpredictability of the adventure life.

The young professionals were friends of my stepsister, who kindly put me up for the evening. Even though everyone was nice, I couldn't help but feel like an interloper. The young professionals were all my age, but they had spouses, mortgages, new cars, and fashionable clothes. The girls had long hair and the guys talked about sports.

I bet they thought I was weird. But if they did, they didn't show it. They asked me questions about my trip, and the general consensus seemed to be, "I respect what you're doing and I could never, ever do it." The feeling was mutual, and that's okay. What if difference doesn't have to mean division?

*

The next morning, I took Lucky to a bike shop to get her chain properly cleaned. On the way, I passed a solid brick building and serious-looking students making their way to class. Philadelphia Community College, read the brass letters above the doors. I let my eyes linger on them for a moment. *Here's a school,* I thought, *where Friday could succeed.*

The quality of his education thus far wouldn't be a liability here. He could meet American students who might relate to him better than the children of privilege who make up so much of the population of Ivy League schools. But there's no financial aid for international students at a place like this. Friday has no choice. He's gotta shoot the moon.

There are 26,000 students at the Community College of Philadelphia. If just $1 were set aside from each of their tuition bills, it would be enough money to cover a full four-year scholarship for a poor student from the African village.

Just a thought.

*

Later that day, I sat in the Bryn Mawr Library computer lab and Googled "SAT."

About The College Board

We're a mission-driven not-for-profit organization that connects students to college success.

Ohh, you're "mission-driven" and "not-for-profit," huh? So then I guess it shouldn't matter that these hard-working students can't afford your $90 test, right? After all, if you made a mandatory test impossible for poor students to afford, well, that's not going to "connect them to college success," now, is it? Friggin corporations.

With a little research, I found a list of college administrators who served on something called the Financial Assistance Assembly. Their job, the website said, was to "define the core strengths and values" of the College Board.

How wonderful! I thought. *I bet they'll be just* delighted *to hear about a way they can improve educational access for needy, talented students!* Their contact information wasn't listed, but it didn't take much Googling to find their work email addresses. And then I set up an online petition.

Let Poor Students Worldwide Take the SAT for Free

No matter how poor they are, international students still have to pay $90 to take the SAT — **36% of the yearly income** for the average Malawian family. That's like telling an American family living on $25,000 per year that they have to cough up $9,000 for the SAT!

To the College Board: There are already so many obstacles standing between deserving but poor students and American universities. Why add another one? How much do you really stand to lose by letting a handful of kids per year take this test for free? Please offer fee waivers to ALL poor students, regardless of nationality.

Every time someone signed my petition, an email would go out to all 21 members of the Financial Aid Assembly. I giggled. How perfectly *annoying!* Imagine if I got 100 people to sign this — there's no *way* the College Board could ignore that!

The next step was to shamelessly spam my Facebook wall.

Hi everybody! Did you know that the SAT doesn't offer fee waivers for international students — even if their families live on less than a dollar per day? That's messed up! Let's see if we can change that. I got nothin going on today, so I'm gonna post this once an hour until I get 100 signatures. Sign and share! Let's change the world!!

It's harder than you'd think to get people to act, even if it's something as easy as signing a petition. After seven hours, I only had 24 signatures. But I refused to let my discouragement win. In the face of indifference, I've found it's best to be relentlessly optimistic. And if people think you're an oblivious idiot, well, let them. You know the battle you're waging.

So I kept bringing the energy, kept showing people I was serious about this. And lo and behold, eight hours in, I started picking up momentum. The number of signatures doubled, and doubled again. We passed 100… without a single peep from the College Board.

100 emails isn't enough for you? I thought. *That's fine. The longer you try to ignore me, the more I'm gonna get in your face.*

Don't let my façade of empty-headed confidence fool you: This was completely humiliating and terrifying. Let's take a look at...

INT. - THE CONTROL PANEL OF MY BRAIN
Maple is grinning maniacally, flipping switches and pushing buttons.

MAPLE
Why yes I *will* spend $4.99 on a clipboard.
We're goin' *old-school* with this!
Stroking her chin.
"Excuse me. Did you know the SAT doesn't offer fee waivers for the children of African subsistence farmers? Could your family afford to spend $9,000 for you to take the SAT?"
Rubbing her hands together.
Oh yeah, that's the good stuff.

Fiddlehead enters. Her eyes widen with alarm and she dashes over to the control panel.

FIDDLEHEAD
AAAAAAAA what are you doing??!?
MAPLE
Changing the world.
FIDDLEHEAD
Throwing herself between Maple and the control panel.
ohhhmygod you are SO embarrassing stop bothering those people, they're busy with real responsibilities and don't have time for your NONSENSE

MAPLE
Easily pushing her aside.
I'm helping them do their jobs. I'm giving them the opportunity to reverse a discriminatory policy.

FIDDLEHEAD
you're not a Peace Corps Volunteer anymore. they'll think you're just some weird crazy person.

MAPLE
What's crazy about trying to make a difference?

FIDDLEHEAD
YOU ARE HOMELESS!!!

MAPLE
I AM RIGHT.

Ten days after I started the petition, I got an email from the College Board director of communications:

Good Afternoon Brooke,

Our members have informed us about your Change.org petition about providing international fee waivers for the SAT. We appreciate and share your commitment to expanding access for low income students around the world. We have some initiatives currently underway that we think will be of interest to you, and would be happy for you to talk with Linda Liu, College Board's Vice President of International, so you can hear more details about these initiatives and so we can hear from you about the ideas you have to improve outcomes for international students.

Please let me know if you are interested and I'd be glad to coordinate a time for you and Linda to chat.

Please feel free to stop emailing our members directly as they are aware of your petition and have done their part in communicating back to us.

I cackled. "Please feel free to stop emailing our members directly" is corporate robot-speak for "You annoyed us and it worked, now knock it off."

It seemed my evil plan to save the world was a success... for now.

*

Patrick and Gina are never going to fix up their house.

First of all, they're never here. Patrick is the captain of a wooden sailing ship — and he's the stable, sedentary one! Gina's off working as a marine tech off the coast of Antarctica.

Second, there's stuff everywhere. Art and antique tools all over the walls, hundreds of books, plants spilling over every windowsill, and how exactly are you going to move that massive model ship in the kitchen?

Third, it's a tremendously ambitious project. They didn't just buy this house — they bought the one behind it too, and converted it into a barn/workshop. You know, for all their *other* carpentry projects — restoring boats, constructing props for cabaret shows, and whatever it is they have planned for that pile of old bicycles.

It's just unrealistic. They're living in a dream...

(... and every dreamer knows that's exactly the point!)

---

diner break: honey's sit 'n eat
(philadelphia, penn.)

The kind of food so nourishing that you feel like a video game character drinking a health potion.

I found myself biking through a poor neighborhood in Philadelphia, and my first thought was to be afraid. My second thought was, *Wow, that's racist.* And my third was, *What if my ex were here?*

Just like with the flat tire, I'd let him take the lead. If he seemed comfortable, I'd relax too. *There's no way I'm a racist*, I'd tell myself. *He's not scared, so I'm not scared, because there's nothing to be scared of.* And if I did detect a note of fear? *Wow, I think he might be a little racist. Does he think he's* protecting *me? Shame on him for not examining his privilege. Let's just get out of this situation as quickly as possible and let the "protector" feel like a hero.*

How's *that* for projection?

But I was alone. There was no one I could blame my feelings on, just a hard truth about myself and a decision that was mine alone to make: Was I going to give in to this moment of prejudice?

Nah. The opposite of fear is friendliness, so I played a game of Smile At Everybody And See How Many People Smile Back.

I'm not going to claim this situation cured me of prejudice. Nor will I argue that women shouldn't be aware of situations where we might be vulnerable. (As it turns out, the neighborhood I was in has one of the highest rates of violent crime in Philadelphia.) But I'll also tell ya this: that was my all-time highest-scoring game of Smile At Everybody and See How Many People Smile Back.

> **how to play Smile at Everybody and See How Many People Smile Back**
> **Step 1**: Smile at everybody.
> **Points**: 1 if the person smiles back.
> 2 if they're attractive.
> 3 if they say hi!
> Takes 1 point to win.

Burlington, N.J.
16 days · 769 miles

Peter's eyes are faraway and misty. He sips red wine and drifts absently around the room, like a balloon in the current of an oscillating fan. Debra and I sit at the table, talking intently about the occult: ghosts, tarot, auras, energy. When I mention

75

that I found a turkey feather earlier that day, she says with authority, "That's auspicious."

It's not every day you meet a real-live psychic, let alone one who buys you pizza and gives you a place to stay!

Debra's hair spills over her shoulders in whorls and corkscrews as intricate as a fingerprint, and behind her black-rimmed glasses, her eyes are bottomless as hot diner coffee. She exudes a powerful energy, like the rush of wind before rain. I sit up straight as she turns her gaze on me, angling her head slightly to the right — the better, I imagine, to peer into the immutable essence of my being.

She seems to like me, and for that I am grateful. If this person likes me, I must be doing something right.

I'm glad Peter likes me too. I'd forgotten we'd met until he opened the door: the nerdy glasses, the graying ponytail, the boyish smile. That's right, Uncle Dean's second funeral[11], the one in New Jersey.

The first funeral centered largely on Jesus, and the mortician shaved off Dean's mustache, combed his hair and put him in a suit. I remember standing over the casket and trying my hardest, but I couldn't summon the tears to mourn this skinny Christian man who bore a passing resemblance to my uncle.

But in Jersey, it was light-hearted. At the reception, I sat at a table with Peter and a bunch of Dean's other friends, and we told rollicking stories and laughed so hard we tilted back in our chairs. From up on a cloud, in a NASA t-shirt with his hair pointing every which way, Uncle Dean raised a root beer in a toast.

Peter is a link to my ancestry, to the memory of my mother's family. He helped her through the death of her father when she was just a teenager. He comforted her when her eldest brother

---

[11] If you knew Dean Powell — whose self-appointed nickname was "Mr. Famous" — you would understand why he had two funerals.

Rich died at age 38, leaving behind his wife and their two young children. He offered support when my grandmother was dying over six long and painful years. And he was there when Dean, the only other remaining member of my mother's family, finally had to go too.

There's the family you're born with and the family you make, and sometimes the family you find. And sometimes life makes a new family for you when your old family leaves you behind.

Abruptly, Peter breaks his dreamy silence. "Debra," he says. "Make her a mojo bag like the one you made for me."

Debra closes her eyes and nods. She rises and glides to a shelf, where she begins selecting from an assortment of crystals, stones, and trinkets. Peter takes her seat and looks at me earnestly.

"When I got my first motorcycle after Debra and I started dating, she made me a mojo bag — like a good-luck charm, to keep me safe. So I carried it in my motorcycle jacket."

Debra, satisfied with her selections, returns to the table. She lays out a cloth.

"And then one day I got rear-ended by a car. I was stopped in traffic, felt the impact. I had enough time in my head to say 'Oh fuck' before the lights went out."

"Oh my god!"

He looks at me intently. "And I got up and walked away."

"You physically got up and walked away?"

He nods. "After I regained consciousness, the EMTs untangled me from my motorcycle and we walked to the ambulance. I had no injuries."

On the cloth, Debra has laid out a small figurine, a folded piece of paper, and three stones. She's gripping a glassy crystal the size of a bar of soap, and uses it to draw fast, tight circles around the cloth. Every so often, she flicks whatever she's gathering off to the side with a grimace of distaste.

"Peter, that's incredible!"

"At the emergency room, the doctor goes, 'You're really lucky.' And I said, 'Yeah, I get that.' He goes, 'No. 1% of the people that get rear-ended on a motorcycle walk away.'"

I am silent.

"It was a miracle."

Debra squints, searching overhead. She's changed her grasp on the crystal, and now she's tracing an ellipse, skimming the air for some nameless, invisible particles, and splashing them down onto the assortment of stones. When she is satisfied, she places them one by one into a small black velvet bag and hands it to me.

"Can I look inside?"

"Yes, of course. The purple is amethyst. It moderates your energy, and repels things that are negative. But it transmutes that energy, and sends it back into the universe in a positive way... And that's black tourmaline. It creates a forcefield of protection. It's my go-to, because for me it's the strongest of the protection stones. The brown one is a tiger-eye, for focus and balance. But it also has protective properties as well. And that's Ganesh, the road opener. He clears away the obstacles."

I unfold the paper. On one side is an illustration of a monk with a ring of curly blonde hair cradling a child in one arm and holding a lily in his free hand.

"Anthony of Padua," Debra says. "He helps you find lost objects, but if you lose your way, he'll guide you."

I replace the charms into the bag and say, simply, "Wow."

"Keep it on your person at all times, and it will protect you from harm."

"That's right," Peter declares.

"Oh, and you can recharge it in the light of the full moon." Debra says this in the same by-the-way tone as when she told me where I could find the bath towels.

In moments like this, "thank you" is a meaningless utterance. Just two empty, oafish syllables. But they will have to do.

"You're welcome," Peter says, and then adds with emphasis. "Be safe. You've got people who love you looking out for you…" He gestures above.

From up on his cloud, with his hair forever pointing every which way, Uncle Dean raises his root beer and smiles.

*

The four-leaf clover, the lucky pink bandana knotted around my handlebars, the turkey feather, and now this mojo bag. Do I actually believe any of this is going to bring me luck or keep me safe?

Well, I haven't read any peer-reviewed studies that prove or disprove the existence of a forcefield of protection created by black tourmaline. And I certainly wouldn't put myself in dangerous situations and think, "Hey, no worries — I'll let my bandana take the heat on this one." But I'd cheer for a marathon runner. Wouldn't you? That's the magic of a good-luck charm, I think. To make you feel like you're not alone, even when you are.

Let's take a closer look at that pink bandana. To a casual observer, it's nothing more than a dingy, tattered rag. But it's one of my most cherished possessions.

Back when I still had an office job and a Honda Civic, back when I lived in a cage I made for myself, I thought being an adult meant I didn't get to go on adventures anymore. But then my sister convinced me to take a road trip.

We drank craft beer in Mobile, ate alligator in New Orleans, got lost in a Mississippi trailer park, became severely dehydrated hiking in the west Texas desert until we found an oasis and dunked our heads in, got into a screaming fight in New Mexico, became convinced zombies were chasing us in Oklahoma, ate fried pies in Nashville, and made our victorious return to Atlanta at 1 a.m. in a cloud of blueberry cigar smoke.

I bought that bandana in Texas, before that thirsty hike on the Mule Ears Trail. Since then, I've carried it on every single adventure I've gone on. It serves as a reminder of the places I've been, that I always turn out okay in the end, and that being an adult means I *absolutely* get to keep going on adventures.

To other people, it's a rag. To me, it's a good-luck charm. And that's magic too.

5
living the dream

After we became friends, I told Evan, "Wanna know my first impression of you? I thought you were a complete asshole. And now I know the truth... you are."

"Aww," he said scathingly.

"What was your first impression of *me*?"

He tilted his head and considered the question. "I have a theory that... some people are born... with a 'kick me' sign on their back."

"HEY!"

"But then I learned that, all appearances to the contrary, you're actually a badass."

"Aww," I said scathingly.

We worked together out at the Willie Field galley at McMurdo, just the two of us, and it was literally this shit for six hours at a time. Actually, that's not true. There were also elaborate pranks and silly games of what was essentially kitchen-themed Calvinball and even the occasional genuine moment. So naturally when I got to his house, he had laid out an extravagant assortment of gifts on my bed along with a note, which read:

*I hope your stay is comfortable**

**Or not, I don't care...*

For your enjoyment, I have provided:

- *A special orthopedic pillow*
- *A towel, in the unlikely event that you choose to shower*
- *Some delightful vegetarian snacks* [Author's note: they were rum bars with like 3,500 calories each]
- *Hot chocolate because I think you might die without it*
- *A rubber band gun so we can have a war*
- *A respirator, in case your own farts are too stinky and threaten to whelm you over in the night*

We went out to dinner, and he didn't even let me look at the menu, just glanced over it with his professional chef's gaze and ordered the three best things they had. He paid with one of those credit cards that's vantablack and weighs two pounds.

The next morning, I went down to the basement to get my clothes out of the dryer, and woke someone up in the basement bedroom. Later, I told Evan, "Oh god, I'm so embarrassed. I think I woke up your tenant this morning."

"That was me, you dullard."

"Oh! I feel so much better. Why do you sleep in the basement, Evan? Is it because you're a troll?"

"I *don't*. You're in *my* bedroom. The ceilings are so low in the basement that I didn't think you could stand up straight."

"EVAN YOU'RE SECRETLY THE NICEST PERSON IN THE WORLD!" I screamed and then I gave him a hug, because he *hates* when I do that.

Evan is an aloof cat that swipes and hisses at strangers, and I am the fool who keeps coming back because DA WIDDWE KITTY WANTS A KISS ON HIS HEAD!!!

But the thing is, the aloof cat really DOES want a kiss on his head. He just has to absolutely trust the person, because his claws are protecting an exceptionally good heart.

*

At UPenn, I met with a tall, thin kid who seemed fresh out of college, with the most perfect suit and bowtie that you ever did see. As we were talking about Malawi and the Peace Corps, he asked, "Do you know Lea Artino?"

I was stunned for a second. "Uh, yeah, she was in my group."

"She was my best friend in college!"

"YOU KNOW LEA?!?!"

Lea was, of course, one of the toughest girls in our group. I share this story with the utmost respect: This girl had diarrhea for the first *six months* of our service. But she just rolled with it, like, "I worked really hard to get here and I'm not going to let this stop me, so let's see who quits first: me or the diarrhea."

And after six months, the diarrhea finally said, "*Jesus*, okay, I *concede*. Girl, you are one stubborn bitch, and that's a compliment."

Anyway, after finding out we had the legendary Lea in common, it was sort of hard to follow the professional script. I knew he could extrapolate from Lea's experience and have a pretty good idea of what kind of person I was. And I knew that anyone who Lea would consider a best friend must have a special strength of character.

Following our meeting, I got on a bus and went to New York City. Why not ride your bike? you might ask. Because, I reasoned, New York is a place where even the cyclists are rude to the cyclists, and as my friend Brandon put it, "it's not a matter of *if* you get hit by a car, it's *how many times* and *how hard.*" My intent was to bus up there, meet with the representative from Columbia, spend a night hanging out with the aforementioned Brandon, then resume my tour on a route that avoided the city.

The best laid plans…

First, my meeting at Columbia was a complete bust. I met with the counselor on duty in the lobby of the admissions building. She had to lead a tour in 15 minutes and kept checking her watch. *Ahh well,* I thought later over a root beer and a giant slice of pizza. *Ya can't win em all At least UPenn was a home run. I still can't believe that coincidence. I mean, what are the odds?*

And then, in a city of nearly 10 million people, waiting at a stoplight on a street corner in Brooklyn, who do I see biking down the street in the opposite direction but another one of my friends from the Peace Corps?

"NO WAY!" I yelled.

Tom's eyes landed on me, and he exploded into a gigantic laugh.

When you travel, you see how big the world is. And how small too.

*

That night, Brandon and I were standing in his backyard, watching his dog run gleefully through the overgrown weeds and chatting with his neighbor over the fence. It would have been a wholesome scene, except we were also smoking a blunt the size of a Tampax.

"You're riding across the country, huh?" the neighbor asked.

"That's the plan."

"Well I got a little present for ya."

He disappeared into his house, reemerged with a mason jar full of homegrown, and then proceeded to hand me a fistful of weed. That's some Brooklyn hospitality right there.

It was a foggy morning in Philadelphia, and it was time for me to push onward. My weekend of ripping on Evan while we gorged ourselves on apple fritters and all-you-can-eat sushi had come to a close. Now it was time for a dreaded Genuine Moment.

"Good luck," he said, looking down at the sidewalk. "I admire what you're doing."

"Thanks for everything, Evan," I mumbled with my shoulders around my ears.

We shrugged and shared a reluctant hug. Later that day, I found $100 that he'd snuck into my tube bag. And later still, the "kick me" sign he'd taped to my back.

*

"Where's home?"

This question is incredibly hard for me to answer. I usually just go with, "I grew up in Vermont." Some people are content with this. But others look at me like I'm just a silly billy and say, "Okay, but where do you live *now*?" Ahh jeez, when did this turn into the census? My two answers are:

"Uhh, nowhere really, I travel a lot." (And then the person thinks I'm dodging the question.)

Or:

"Most recently, [insert location]." (And then the person thinks I'm a liar because the most recent location of late has been a research base in Antarctica.)

Can ya tell it makes me self-conscious? It's a totally innocuous question; people want to know where they can ground you. But what if you're rootless? In a society where structure gives us meaning, people who exist across boundaries — nomads, drifters, vagabonds — are less civilized, maybe even deviant.

What is home anyway? In the West, we use it as shorthand for "the place where you live," but that's not exactly accurate. If someone's asking directions to your house, your home is an address. But take a cross-country road trip, and suddenly your home is a state. Get on a plane and cross an ocean, and home becomes an entire country.

You can feel at home in a lot of places: your parents' house, your favorite café, your tent on the side of the road in a town you've never been. And you can live in a place you don't consider your home — just ask a refugee, a hostage, a prisoner.

Or a lonely old woman in a nursing home.

I'm standing on the sidewalk outside your house in Metuchen, New Jersey, and your ghost is floating at my shoulder.

I can't believe they painted it that hideous yellow, you say.

The red was nicer, I think.

It looks like dog piss, you snap, and I smile. This was your home.

I remember treasures decorating every shelf, every windowsill, and every inch of the walls. I remember the green shag carpet, the smell of marinara bubbling on the stove, and the sound of some old movie on the TV. I remember nighttime, the streetlamp through the window, and a room filled with moonlight and the hum of an oscillating fan and the mewling of a far-off siren. The headlights of passing cars cast sliding squares of light along the walls. I didn't know what to call them, so I called them skeletons. I was a kid from the country, and I'd never seen so many skeletons in my entire life.

And I remember you, in your slippers and your housecoat and your platinum-blonde hair. You painted watercolor landscapes and threw stuff when you were pissed off and whenever a waitress asked how you were doing, you'd say, "Anyone I can, honey."

Dolores Powell: grandmother, artist, force of nature.

I get why Mom moved you to Raleigh; you couldn't take care of the house anymore. But you were never the same. It reminded me of the babushkas of Chernobyl. Did you ever hear this story? After the nuclear disaster — which released *400 times* the radiation as the bombing of Hiroshima — everyone was relocated. But a handful of people, mostly tough old broads like you, kept coming back. The government couldn't keep them out, so they figured, well, these are old ladies, let em live out the last few years of their lives wherever they want.

The ones who came back to Chernobyl ended up outliving the ones who didn't. That's a beautiful truth, isn't it? Stubborn old ladies are more powerful than nuclear radiation.

But you lost that power when you moved to Raleigh. Without your social networks, your connection to your environment, you were a prisoner. You left your home for an apartment, and left that apartment for a room in an old folk's home, and then you left this world for the next.

I am standing alone on the sidewalk outside a home I can't enter. I am a ghost.

I think back on all the places I've lived. The ramshackle farmhouse where I grew up, the 16 acres that surrounded it. The muddy pond where we swam in the summer, the frozen hills we'd sled down in the winter, the milkweed field we'd tear through in the fall, sending thistledown drifting into the crisp air against a backdrop of flaming foliage. My mom sold that house when I was 19; now it's a cold haunted place I only visit in the perpetual twilight of my dreams.

The hunter-green Hennessey Hammock where I slept on the Appalachian Trail. The apartment Jill and I shared in Ithaca that always smelled like lavender from the aromatherapy studio downstairs. My house in Chikweo, the cool concrete floor and the doorway where I would lean and watch the sunset. All these places I've lived and loved, all these places I can never return.

"Where's home?" people ask me.

Nowhere, I think turning away from my grandmother's old house.

And I drift away, as detached and insignificant as a wisp of milkweed fuzz on the breeze.

*

All I want is to be a hobo, I declared.

You'll change your mind, he told me.

No way, man. The open road, waking up in a different place every day, meeting people and hearing their stories…

Women have a biological clock, he told me.

Not me! I asserted. I long to escape this oppressive society that punishes its intelligent youth with AP classes. I just want to pack a bag and go, take off into the wild, windy night and see how far I get.

You'll see, he told me. Once you get to your 30s, your priorities will change.

His name was Samar, and he was a member of an online message board I used to frequent when I was a teenager. This was back in the days of dialup; back when the internet was a scary, almost transgressive place; back in the days before we had a term for what he was doing, which was, of course, mansplaining.

I loved it. In my little internet community, I got a chance to talk to adults who actually took me seriously, who debated with me and helped me understand the world a little better. Which is why Samar's assertion scared me so much. Was there something he knew that I didn't?

But now here I was in my 30s, and my priorities hadn't changed. My 16-year-old self would be elated to learn that I'd actually figured out a way to live my dream. And I also just so happened to be passing through Samar's neighborhood! I sent him a Facebook message asking if he'd be interested in catching up, and soon we were sitting at a little outdoor table in Princeton, sipping coffee and talking about what happened to the old gang from the message board.

I think he was impressed with how I'd turned out. He knew me when I was a teenager from a small town, reaching out to the wider world and trying to articulate my dreams. Who could have predicted that this is where we'd be 16 years later?

Once the gossip ran out, the conversation meandered to future plans.

"I'm trying to get another contract to go back to Antarctica," I said. "I love it down there. And then maybe hike the Pacific Crest Trail? I want to get to South America and Australia within the next couple years, and Hawaii. And I'd love to live in a van, or maybe go tiny house if I find the right place. Though I really can't imagine settling down."

"What about a family?" he asked.

I think I yelled "Barf!" or something equally sensitive and nuanced.

"You'll change your mind," he said, and inwardly my eyes widened. *Oh my god… is he actually going to say it?*

In a tone of gentle concern, he said, "Women have a biological clock. You'll see. Your priorities will change"

Oh my god he's saying it! The exact same words and everything!

He looked over my shoulder, squinting a little, as if to make out something dim and far away. "Take it from me. I'm almost 50, and I'm… alone. I see my friends, my siblings and their kids, and the fulfillment they get from their families. It's the most fulfilling thing we can do as human beings… Don't get me wrong, I think your life is remarkable," he said, and met my eye. "But you might want to consider sharing the adventure."

In actually *hearing* it, in the subtlety of his tone and the ache in his gaze, those words that held such power over me for so long clattered lifelessly to the ground. Samar wasn't a mansplainer, and he wasn't privy to some wisdom I hadn't yet accessed. He was just a guy with a good heart who'd mistaken his own dream for mine.

snapshots: new jersey

Princeton's regal campus melts away into a muddy gravel towpath running alongside a river. Turtles line the logs and turn their little heads up to the sun. A heron takes wing at my approach.

I thought Jersey was supposed to be the armpit of America?

*

An abandoned lot run through with cracks like a concrete patchwork quilt stitched with hardy tufts of grass.

In the end, plants always win.

*

But also and of course, NJ 35 and 36, and a frightened biker pedaling alongside cars screaming past at 50 mph, telling herself to be brave.

Middletown, N.J.
21 days · 901 miles

The plan: Hop on the ferry and bike through New York in the middle of the day, thus avoiding rush hour and making it to my Warm Showers in Connecticut by nightfall.

The reality: Get wrapped up in a deep conversation with the quietest guy on the Appalachian Trail[12] at the Jersiest diner in all of Jersey[13] and miss my ferry by six minutes.

---

[12] His Trail name was *Chatterbox*, that's how quiet he was.

[13] It had a life-size statue of Elvis Presley ushering patrons toward the bathroom!

I slunk out of the terminal, the picture of defeat. The next ferry didn't leave for *four more hours*, which would put me in New York at 5 o'clock on the dot. I had to reschedule my Warm Showers in Connecticut, find a place to sleep in the city, navigate rush hour traffic, and figure out how I was gonna kill the long afternoon ahead of me.

The bike path cut through a swath of tall, golden grass that opened up to a rocky shoreline. I took off my shoes and put on my sweatshirt and walked barefoot through the cool sand, the sloshing, foamy water and New York in the foggy distance like a faded lithograph or a dream half-remembered. Back in the diner, I'd asked Chatterbox his favorite emotion. He thought deeply before he gave me his answer.

"In Japan, there's this concept called monoaware," he said quietly. "There's no English word for it, but it translates to the bittersweet melancholy that comes from the realization that nothing is permanent, that everything one day will pass."

So I missed the ferry, I thought. *There are worse ways to spend an afternoon than hanging out on a beach.*

And worse ways to spend an evening than in a gay piano bar on the Upper East Side catching up with a friend you haven't seen in 10 years. Brandon offered me his couch again, but he was working late, so I posted on Facebook and asked if anyone wanted to hang out with me for the evening. Much to my surprise, Steve got in touch.

Memory's a tricky bitch. When I looked back at the time I spent with Steve, I remembered asking him ignorant questions about being gay and stirring up awkward drama among our group of friends at the student newspaper. Also, I once went to see him play an open mic and wore a shirt that said "Steve Rocks My Vagina." (In my defense, it was his idea.) I could only imagine that was what he remembered too, and I wasn't sure what he hoped to get out of an evening with me.

But we ended up having a great time. Conversation was easy, and covered everything from linguistics to STDs, sexuality, politics, and everything we'd been up to over the last decade. At the end of the night, he told me he was inspired by what I was doing and wanted more people like me in his life.

"Thanks," I said. "To be honest, I was kind of surprised you even wanted to hang out. I guess, I dunno, I'd like to take this opportunity to apologize for being so rude to you back in college."

He looked at me thoughtfully and said, "Brooke, I remembered you as kind."

*

Sometimes you're thrust headfirst into a situation you have done everything in your power to avoid. Like, for example, rush hour in New York City.

"Rise and shine, sleepyhead!" I heard Brandon say.

"Buhh," I grunted groggily, and then shot up. It was totally light out. "What time is it??"

"8:22."

"Noooooooooooo," I whined. "How does a 6'2 human sharing a couch with a snoring pitbull *oversleep*?"

"It's improbable," Brandon grinned. "But you found a way."

"Brandon, what time does rush hour end?"

"… Never?" he offered. Clearly he didn't understand the gravity of the situation. I hadn't ridden my bike in a city in years. How was I going to survive rush hour in the biggest, angriest city in America?

Brandon's wife, perhaps hearing the cataclysmic despair in my voice, offered her thoughts on the situation: a wide-legged shuffle out of their room in a bra and underwear, snapping her hands like a crab trying to impress a mate, singing, "Naaaaaaaked! Naked naked naked naked naaaaaaaaaaked!"

Lulu made an excellent point. I was taking this *way* too seriously. Just yelling at myself to do the damn thing doesn't do anything except make me hate my life. And I *hate* hating my life — it's the only one I've got! I had two options: Quit or do it. And one of those options wasn't an option. So I put on the *Hamilton* soundtrack[14] and dove into rush hour traffic.

Two and a half hours later, as the final chords of the soundtrack rang out, I'd only just made it to the Bronx. New York is friggin endless. But by that point it was clear I'd gotten worked up over nothing. New York may be big and mean, but it also has bike lanes.

*

A long denim skirt with a white lace hem dragging in the sand. That old tomboy, the Atlantic.

The sun and I were totally in sync: Every time I thought I might want to put on another layer, he'd pop out from behind a cloud and bake the outside of my windbreaker. As soon as I started to sweat, he'd duck behind another cloud.

What is freedom?

Hanging out with the sun.

The bike path veered sharply left, and suddenly my view was not of the humbling immensity of the ocean, but of the bumbling shortsightedness of man. Fences and walls and NO TRESPASSING signs. Ahh yes, the 1%. Leave it to the rich to see a good thing, decide they own it, and then ruin it. It was almost funny, how much they had missed the point. Like the house I

---

[14] If a bastard orphan son of a whore and a Scotsman dropped in the middle of a forgotten spot in the Caribbean by providence impoverished in squalor can grow up to be a hero and a scholar, surely I can ride a bicycle for a few hours without dying.

Also, for those of you who might question the wisdom of listening to music while biking on crowded city streets, all I have to say is, "Can't hear ya, I got headphones in."

passed with a sign that said NO TRESPASSING underneath another sign that said NO TRESPASSING.

I tried to imagine what it must have looked like before all these rich people came here with their NO TRESPASSING signs. I bet it was communal. I bet it was a place of worship.

I passed a sign warning me that I was on camera, and made a jerking-off motion at it.

I saw a bloated building that sprawled over a hillside like mold growing on a piece of birthday cake. It was easily the size of my high school, maybe bigger. *Maybe it's a hotel!* thought my inner optimist. *Or like... a spiritual retreat?*

My ass, thought my inner pessimist.

I saw a runner in the distance, and when I got close, I called out, "Excuse me — is that a hotel or a house?"

"That's a house!" he laughed. "A little over-the-top, wouldn't ya say?"

"Unbelievable!" I said with a laugh, but inside I was fuming. In Malawi, people build their own houses out of mud bricks they bake in the sun and grass they harvest from the fields. All this in addition to the normal schedule of farming, carrying 60 liters of water from the borehole on their heads, doing chores, raising their children, and going to school. Their houses are utilitarian structures that keep them dry when it rains and warm when it's cold; living is done outside.

Did this person work harder for this eyesore of a status symbol than someone who built their house themselves while also struggling just to get enough food to eat? Would anyone argue that this person worked harder than any average woman living in an African village?

I reached a little shopping center and popped into a deli for a cup of coffee and that most marvelous of emotional panaceas: a giant chocolate chip cookie.

"Do you have a bathroom?" I asked, and the guy told me there was one in the diner next door.

Well damn. If I'd known there was a diner, I would have gone there in the first place. I hate using the bathroom without buying anything; I'm pretty sure it's one of the cardinal sins of the service industry. But I *really* had to pee... The two old ladies working the counter scowled but didn't say anything.

I shouldn't have pushed my luck. I should have just gone back to the deli. What was I thinking when I asked if they would mind filling up my water bottles?

"Are you going to *buy* anything?" demanded one.

"We let you use the bathroom, that's enough," said the other bitingly.

Wounded, I left.

My trip thus far had been marked by such kindness and generosity, and this was a rude reminder that people aren't always nice. "Hurt people hurt people," the saying goes, and that's exactly where I was at. I fumed and thought about all the mean things I could say to make those women feel the same embarrassment and shame as I felt. *You're the same kind of selfish as that person in that sickening house. How hard would it be for you to spare a little water? I'm biking across the country to help African college students, for fuck's sake – I'm a* saint!

I took a breath and laughed at myself. *Okay there, Saint Brooke, let's look at it from their point of view. Some sweaty chick walks in and uses the bathroom and asks for water and doesn't buy anything, yeah, that's annoying. They're probably tired and feel powerless and took it out on you, but it's nothing personal. I bet if they knew you and what you were doing, they'd help you. And it's in the past, so leave it there.*

It drives me nuts sometimes, how fucking sensible I can be. Especially when I'm not ready to stop feeling like crap.

I passed a restaurant further up the road, and the guy bussing the patio tables looked up at me and met my eye. He smiled.

I'm sure it was a reflex, just what people in the service industry do when they make eye contact. Or maybe he was playing Smile At Everybody And See How Many People Smile Back. But it startled me out of my black cloud. I smiled back, and immediately felt better.

"Oh, that's right!" I thought. "Basic human kindness!"

Yale
29 days · 1,012 miles

"We had a student from the Kakuma refugee camp who was exceptionally bright, truly gifted," Dana told me. "We had no doubt he could keep up academically, but we were concerned that he wouldn't be able to hit the ground running, coming straight from a refugee camp to..." She gestured around her.

"Understandably so."

"So we secured funding for him to repeat his senior year at a private school here in New Haven."

"Really?!"

She smiled. "That way he could get used to American culture, the different education system, get all those growing pains out of the way in a safe environment."

"That's above and beyond anything I've ever heard of a college doing for a needy international student."

"It was certainly a special case. But we felt he had potential, and we wanted to fully nurture that potential. We're not in the business of setting people up to fail. I only wish we could do that for more students. But as it stands..." She paused and sighed.

"I get it," I said. "There's only so much money to go around. It's just unfortunate that students from Africa are expected to basically be superheroes in order to be taken seriously by admissions departments. No offense."

"None taken, it's definitely an issue. Believe me, I think what you're doing is admirable, and if I had my choice, we'd admit many more students from backgrounds like Friday's."

"It's so comforting to hear you say that. The more people I talk to, the more I realize that that's what admissions counselors want. To create a well-rounded education for *everyone*, which means a wide array of voices."

She nodded.

"It just seems like… your hands are tied."

She nodded again.

*

The bike trail is a featureless brown ribbon running through the tangle of gaunt springtime trees; an eraser dragged through a pencil sketch on a paper bag. At this time of year, the land looks at once old and young, like the wrinkled head of a baby bird.

The eraser smudge turns into a clean strip of concrete extending toward the vanishing point. A graphite scribble of forest surrounds the marsh, matted grass the color of a weathered old telephone pole. The sun calls its warmth across a vast distance. A few reeds stick out of the water like pins in a silk dress.

The path crosses a still silver river that hugs the brown curves of earth and reflects the sky like a mirror. And then it ducks back into the woods, between great mossy rocks and beneath thorny branches adorned with white apple blossoms.

When I'm cold, I put on a jacket; when I'm hungry, I eat; when I have to pee, an outhouse materializes and I use it. My needs met, I get back on my bike and continue to ride, smiling at the picturesque world around me.

A dream doesn't come true when it concludes. It comes true in moments like these, when it takes you to the unfamiliar places you've always wanted to go.

*

Connecticut College was a lackluster meeting, one that felt more like an interview than a conversation, where my sincerity was met with a tight smile and an answer from the FAQ page. Ah well.

The ride there and back was cool, at least: a path through the woods, past a tree someone hung a painting on, leading to a bridge over the Thames River and a railroad switchyard. Corrugated tin structures crouched over piles of sand and stone, lumber and concrete arranged in stacks, and litter like breadcrumbs following the tracks. Trucks and junk trucks and piles of scrap, dead grass and the earth scraped open like a bleeding cuticle.

It was the kind of industrialization that's so ugly it's poignant; the sort of place that, if abandoned, Nature would reclaim in a matter of years. Vain symbols of a trivial creature howling its significance up at the immense, empty sky.

*

And now here I am in the middle of the woods balancing on a log and dragging my beloved bicycle through a swamp. The only sign of humanity out here is a rusty husk of a car. It is upside down and was clearly set on fire at some point.

"I am so sorry Lucky," I moan as the diarrhea-colored water sloshes over her chain and derailleur. "I love you so much and this is how I treat you because I am a stubborn fool."

If Lucky could talk, she'd probably say something patient and understanding, like, "This is just part of the adventure." And what does Mapsy have to say for himself?

"Continue. straight. on. Un-named For-est Ser-vice Road."

Back when the road was still paved — it felt like miles ago, but of course there's no way to check the map because I have no service on this unnamed forest service road — Mapsy insisted this was a good idea.

"Go. Straight," Mapsy said.

The only thing in front of me was a Dead End sign. "Straight *where*?"

"Go. Straight."

I squinted past the sign at a rough trail cut into the forest.

"On that unnamed forest service road?" I asked.

"Go. Straight."

This should have been a red flag, but I figured Mapsy knew what he was talking about. After a mile or so, the rocks in the road became too big and jagged to bike over, but I told myself I'd gone too far to turn back. After another mile or so, the mud puddles got so big they were basically small ponds, but I told myself I had to be getting toward the end of this road. And now, however many miles in, the road is a swamp and there's a car that looks like it was sacrificed in some sort of dark ritual, and I have reached the limit of my ability to rationalize.

Sometimes you tell yourself you're in too deep to turn back, and sometimes you get to find out what that really means.

*

After getting the brush-off at Columbia, I was a little wary of talking to the counselor on duty at Brown. It was such a gamble. When the counselor knew I'd biked there from Raleigh, it gave me more legitimacy, but with an on-duty counselor, it was like, "Hi! You don't know me, but I'm riding a bike across the country to help a student from when I was a Peace Corps Volunteer! Really! You have to believe me: My credentials are that I'm a complete stranger who just walked into this building!"

But Connie was an absolute delight, a live wire of a woman with a contagious smile and a passion for travel. We swapped tales of the places we'd visited and spoke passionately about the injustice of denying education to the poor.

"It's one of those privileges that we take for granted in America," I mused. "If you're smart and work hard in school, you can go to college. But it's not true everywhere. Even if you do everything right, you still might end up toiling in the fields. Not to say that farming isn't a fine way to make a living, but... think of all that lost potential, the unique perspectives those great minds could have contributed, all for the want of money."

Connie shook her head sympathetically.

"Even if you do go to school, the quality of education in Malawi just isn't the same as America. And you're scraping up the money as you go, so it might take you a decade to finish a four-year degree. By that point, you're set in your ways. But an American education? Getting to Friday's mind while it's still malleable? It would be an opportunity for him to live up to his full potential."

At the end of our meeting, Connie gave me a smile and said, "I'm a hugger — can I give you a hug?"

"Of course! I'm a hugger too!"

"I love your mission and your passion!" she said. "I can't wait to tell my kids about you!"

*

A well-meaning but creepy older guy cornered me in the parking lot of the Bliss Diner. I think he was just curious, but he also had a weird laugh and kept touching my elbow and offering to drive me to Boston.

Gals, you know how we're taught from a young age that it's a scary world, and there are scary people out there? Well, this is what one of them looks like. If you can just... you know... not get into his car, you'll be fine.

Take it from me, the world really isn't as dangerous as everyone tries to convince us it is.

Boston, Mass.
35 days · 1,255 miles

The first sign that MIT wasn't going to work out was... well, the MIT sign.

Whenever I visited a college, I'd lean Lucky up against a sign with the college's name and post it on social media. But the only sign I could find for MIT was MASSACHUSSETTS INSTITUTE OF TECHNOLOGY carved in Roman script across the length of an entire building. The only way I could fit this ridiculously long name into frame with Lucky was to crouch on the sidewalk, while stressed-out students and professors flowed around me, shooting me irritated glances for slowing them down on their way to somewhere actually important.

I think I got "ASSACUSSETS INSTITUTE OF TECHNO" and called it good enough.

I got into the office and steeled myself up for a meeting with the counselor on duty. But like Connie, he was all right. He commented on my Vermont tattoo; turns out he was a Green Mountain Boy himself. When I told him about my trip, his response was: "That's cool." The way he said it sounded conclusive, like an indisputable fact. That seemed to be his mode of communication. No fluff, no euphemisms, no monkey pretending to be a robot.

"Do you offer a bridge program?"

"No."

"Gotcha. What can you tell me about standardized testing requirements?"

"They have to score high, especially in the math and science sections. We require the TOEFL, SAT, and SAT II Subject Tests."

"Aha. And their grades?"

"Mostly A's. 90 to 95% A's."

I put down my pen and said, "Wow."

He shrugged. "Look, we want diversity as much as anywhere else, but at the end of the day, it's MIT."

I got it. And I appreciated the complete lack of bullshit.

From there, I fought my way through Boston traffic to Harvard's flawless campus. I was set to meet Jake, who I'd known through email since my Peace Corps days. Before today, he was a name in my email inbox that I read in the dusty early morning light in the Form 4 classroom, back when I was first researching the feasibility of full scholarships for international students. It felt so legit to say, "Good to finally meet you!"

Our meeting was casual. He sprawled on a couch and rattled off information that I scrawled in my journal as fast as I could keep up. Interesting though our conversation was, I didn't feel like Friday had much of a chance here either. At the end of the day, it is Harvard. And it got me thinking.

It's been this way since I was in high school, and maybe even before that: Teenagers are expected to do it all. A diverse assortment of extracurriculars, every AP class your high school offers, good grades, high standardized test scores, community service, and an after-school job. You're cultivating your résumé before you even *have* a résumé.

But this push toward creating "well-rounded students" might have an unintended consequence: fostering a shitty values system.

In response to a 2016 survey that found American high school students prioritized their own happiness and achievement over caring for others, a group of admissions officers from several elite universities took a step back. Maybe, they thought, this ideal of a "well-rounded" student was actually just a narrowly defined definition of excellence. Maybe what the world of higher education needs is fewer juggling acts and more genuinely good people. To that end, they led a campaign called Turning the Tide that emphasized quality over qualifications.

Wanna know where people still care about each other?

Malawi.

Friday doesn't have a long list of extracurricular activities because there aren't extracurricular activities in rural Malawian schools. But he helped his family with the garden. He tutored his younger sisters when they were having trouble in school. He stood up for his mom when his father tried to leave her for another woman. He lent a hand when he saw strangers carrying heavy loads, offered conversation to other people waiting at the bus stop, shared his food when his friends didn't have enough, respectfully greeted his elders, and reached out to his old English teacher over Facebook messenger, just to see how she was doing and let her know she was missed.

He did this because in Malawi, people look out for each other. Kuyenda awiri si mantha, they say. Traveling together, we cannot be afraid. Malawian culture is formulated around the idea that humans are part of a community first and individuals second. Maybe that's why, despite being one of the poorest countries in the world, it's also one of the most peaceful. In this age of frequent mass shootings, couldn't America stand to learn from a culture like this? And at an institution where America's future leaders are educated, couldn't Friday's perspective be a valuable resource in the search for peace?

*

Ryan and I sat sipping weak tea on the floor of his living room. I needed a shower and he was still in his work clothes, but we were too absorbed in our ultra-leftwing conversation to do anything about it.

"If anything, Bernie Sanders isn't liberal *enough*," he mused.

I love talking to people with different beliefs: the delicate balancing act of respect and honesty, and the satisfaction of finding common ground. But boy oh boy do I also love talking to a fellow liberal. The one conversation is like carefully baking a cake for an honored guest; the other is sharing a pint of Ben & Jerry's.

I floated all my wacky theories about anarchy and economic resistance and education and luck. Ryan met it all thoughtfully, like he'd also spent long hours pondering the same things. We were two people focused not on the world's problems, but on emerging solutions. By the end of our conversation, we'd exchanged handwritten lists of book recommendations.

"How do you feel about breakfast for dinner?"

"I *love* breakfast for dinner!"

"It's one of the best three-word phrases in the English language!"

"I'd rather hear 'breakfast for dinner' than 'I love you!'"

Later that night, over cage-free eggs and organic, local vegetables, we continued the conversation with his roommate and his girlfriend. It felt like an alternate reality, what might have happened had I actually pursued that Ph.D. in cultural anthropology. (Which was the plan back in grad school before I started traveling and realized I'm actually just a no-account drifter.)

This could have been my life. These could have been my friends. This could have been how we spent our evenings, sitting around and talking about all the ways we were going to change the world.

The next morning, I woke up early and was just about to tiptoe out when Ryan came out of his room.

"Oh, I'm so sorry, did I wake you up?"

"No, not at all," he said sleepily. "I just wanted to say it was really nice meeting you, and we should keep in touch."

"Absolutely," I said, and we hugged goodbye.

He went back inside and I headed north, along the narrow streets of his neighborhood, through a park and a back lot and to a main thoroughfare with a roomy bike lane that would eventually take me to Tufts. And I thought:

What if everyone you knew was a melody? Each person with their own time signature, key, instrumentation, theme; with beginnings and endings, patterns and evolution, a story to tell. With some of them you might harmonize, and I suppose you could call that love. Others might be dissonant, but what's life without a little discord?

I found harmony with Ryan and his friends, but then I moved on. I'm always moving on. My family so far away, my friendships so temporary, sometimes even just an evening. In their symphonies I'm a faint pianissimo, a measure or two of music, and then a fermata suspended over a rest. The melody of a traveler is a solo no one else can hear.

*

I got to Tufts early, and when I saw someone walking across the quad, I asked, "Excuse me. Where can I get a cup of coffee around here?"

"I'm actually on my way to the coffee shop. I can show you — it's a little complicated."

"Oh, thanks so much! So, do you work here?"

"I do. I'm the dean of international admissions."

!

Wouldn't ya know it, I came up with the perfect response...
             ... in Indiana!

That's the downside of a long bike tour: All those long, interrupted, lonely hours are the perfect environment for agonizing over every mistake and missed opportunity.

I sputtered something stupid about my trip and Friday, she said something polite about looking forward to his application, and then we walked in awkward silence through a labyrinth of hallways. She was right; it was a little complicated.

Ya can't win em all. At least my proper meeting went well.

"Can you tell me about your testing requirements?" I asked, bright-eyed, bushy-tailed, and adequately caffeinated. "Do you accept the IELTS or DuoLingo? And how much do SATs factor in?"

Matt smiled proudly. "Tufts doesn't have a standardized testing requirement."

I put down my pen. "You're kidding."

"Nope."

"THAT IS INCREDIBLE."

"I KNOW."

And then two geeks sat in a room and geeked out over a topic obscure even by geek standards: standardized testing requirements.

"It's preposterous to ask a kid from the village to take a *Scantron test*."

"Right! Think about how weird that answer sheet would look if you hadn't been taking these tests since you were a kid."

"Even the motion of filling in the bubble —"

"*Right?*"

"Native English speakers fail the TOEFL."

"Right. Kids in the village have no exposure to this level of English. Only the wealthy can afford tutors and classes — not that they don't also work hard —"

"No, of course, but the student from the village who speaks proficient English does so *in spite of* his teachers, and that's arguably a more impressive accomplishment."

"Ohh my god, I'm *so* glad to hear you say that!"

"The IELTS costs $200. That's a *fortune* to a subsistence farmer."

"It's like $2/3$ of their yearly income!"

"And fee waivers are only available through programs like EducationUSA."

"And it's great that those programs exist, but they only have one location. At least in Malawi it's somewhat centrally located and fairly easy to get to. What about a huge country like Zambia?"

"Exactly!"

It was all so perfect. Here was a school that understood the limitations Friday was facing, that seemed to have a place for him, and that understood that he could be a resource, not just a charity case. And their mascot is an *elephant*.

I walked out of the admissions office and felt a bolt of energy shoot through me. *This is it*, I thought. *Tufts. Friday's going to go to Tufts.*

---

diner break: renée's café (medford, mass.)

The smell of coffee and patches of warm sunlight on sand-colored wood.

Ipswitch, Mass.
36 days · 1,316 miles

It was a cool, foggy day in Ipswitch, a place whose claim to fame is being the birthplace of Jonathan Richman. You might know him as the guitarist in the cut scenes of that perennial classic *There's Something About Mary*. His music is basically punk rock's friendly older brother: basic chord progressions played on an acoustic guitar with endearing lyrics about affection or riding the bus or his mother's death or how he's a little airplane.

Tom Waits once said that everything you absorb, you ultimately secrete. If that's the case, was there something about Ipswitch that contributed to Jonathan Richman's aesthetic? If so, I wanted those good vibes on my side while I had my phone conversation with the Director of International Affairs for the

College Board. Passing the local scoop shop, I decided I also wanted ice cream.

On the back deck, over a cup of vanilla soft-serve with rainbow sprinkles (just like a real adult!), Linda told me what I already knew.

"We work with EducationUSA to provide fee waivers to needy students."

"What about the funding gap? The liaison I've been speaking to has been telling me there's no money for months, and it's unclear when there might be more."

"Actually, the Educational Testing Service provides the funds for testing."

"Oh! In that case, do you have any idea when the funding might come through?"

"I can't speak to that, no."

Hrm.

"I'm curious: Why not just offer waivers to students directly?"

She paused and chose her words carefully. "Without some sort of process to assess a student's means, there's too much of a chance that waivers might be abused. I believe you, and I believe that Friday comes from a needy background, but not everyone is that honest. EducationUSA is our way of making sure the waivers make it into the right hands, even if it is a flawed way of addressing the issue."

Flawed is right. If there's only one EducationUSA office in the country and it's in the capital city, it's only accessible to students who live near the capital city. So… not the rural poor. Not the very people for whom the program is designed.

I was deflated. I'd been hoping the conversation would go a little more like this:

Linda: We had no idea our policy was so discriminatory! We'll change it immediately.

Brooke: Fabulous!

Linda: I'm going to go ahead and email you a waiver for Friday. And some supplementary study materials while I'm at it!

Brooke: Thank you so much.

Linda: Have you ever considered a career with the College Board? We could use a passionate visionary like you to guide our international admissions policy.

Brooke: I'm flattered, but I've actually just accepted a position at McMurdo Station in the supply department. Any way I could start after that contract ends?

Instead I just felt like an annoying weirdo who'd just wasted everybody's time. But at least we had an option.

*

With college enrollment down 2 million students since 2011, we may be witnessing a shift in higher education in America. Why could this be?

The price tag is one factor. According to the National Center for Education Statistics, the average public university costs nearly $25,000 per year for students living on-campus (it's a little less expensive if you live at home), and private schools charge more than twice that. Although state spending on public colleges and universities has recently seen an increase, it's still almost $9 billion less than in 2008. The average student loan debt is around $30,000. Even a teenager who's never lived on their own can recognize that starting out their career $30,000 in the hole probably isn't the best investment.

Especially since bachelor's degrees don't guarantee jobs the way they used to. Unless you're in a handful of specialized fields, you gotta shell out even more money for a master's. Gone are the days of getting out of school, getting a job, and working your way up through your company; these days, careers are fluid. Skilled trades and the service industry can be more lucrative, require less of a financial investment, and actually let workers use their bodies, rather than forcing them into a cubicle (or one of those dreadful "open offices") under fluorescent lighting for 40 years.

But back to the sea change in higher education...

Even with tuition rates as high as they've been in American history, less enrollment means less revenue, which means colleges have to make budget cuts. Student programs are among the first to go, which makes the school less attractive to prospective students, further hurting enrollment. The next area to make budget cuts in institutions of higher learning? You guessed it, instructors' salaries! As of 2017, four-year colleges devoted *less than a third* of their revenue to instruction. (On the bright side, some reports say private schools spend 48% of tuition revenue on financial aid. On the not-so-bright side, this also includes athletic scholarships, which doesn't exactly do much to help poor African students.)

In 1969, nearly 80% of college faculty was tenure or tenure track. But as of 2018, that number dropped to less than 30%. These days, adjuncts step in to fill the gap — a bargain for universities, costing an average of $79,000 less per year than a tenured professor. (And at the schools where Friday was applying, closer to $179,000 less.) Adjuncts make a measly $25,000 per year. That's a shade over minimum wage. That's, if you'll remember from earlier in this rant, $5,000 less than the average student loan debt.

They should become administrators instead. Between 1998 and 2003, salaries for university administrators and bureaucrats have increased by 50%. And the median salary for the president of a college is $276,727.

Maybe the current generation is finally waking up to this scam. Your teachers and parents expect you to know what you want to do with your life at age 16. They promise you a future, but they're actually just chaining you to a system.

But in Malawi, a bachelor's degree still means something. And one from America? It's a golden ticket. It opens doors to high-paying jobs with nonprofits, NGOs, media, possibly even the government (although boy oh boy is the government in Malawi corrupt).

What if you educated a student who grew up in the village, who had real ties to that place, friends and neighbors and family? Who had a deep understanding of how the village works, and how it could work better? What if you gave them a hand, pulled them up to a level of society where their ideas were validated and they had access to a powerful array of resources?

Change. Change might happen.

6

is it hard to ride your bike across the country?

Durham, N.H.

37 days · 1,352 miles

Every day is the same on a bike tour: You move forward. The scenery around you blends like watercolors until you realize you're in New England, which is a quite different thing than Pennsylvania, or noble, tangled Virginia before it. And you'll be surprised down the road to find yourself in the Midwest, in the desert, in the mountains, and, if you are tenacious and lucky enough, you will look around and blink and find that you have arrived at your destination.

Of course, you can't think about that, not in the beginning, not even in the middle. You aim for the horizon, no further. You'll never get there, of course, and that's exactly the point.

*

I made it to the drawbridge just as the warning lights started flashing and settled in for a long wait. On the sidewalk next to me stood an older dude with hair like a dandelion seed and a comfortable slump in his shoulders, like he didn't take posture or life too seriously.

"Hate to be stuck up there right now," he said.

And thus began one of those conversations that most people have probably learned how to avoid: lonely kook wants someone to talk at. This sort of thing used to irritate me, but somewhere along the line I realized that it's actually a special gift to listen as a fellow human shares their story with you. Sure, this guy was a little unraveled, but so is my favorite orange sweater. Besides, the road ahead of us was literally lifted 135 feet into the air; where could I go? So I listened.

We had a lot in common, actually. He was rootless in his 20s — big ol backpack, worn-out shoes. He hitchhiked when he could and walked when he couldn't, and stretched his money thin as single-ply toilet paper. These days he was too old to travel, he said almost apologetically, and then added, "But I walk between two and seven hours a day."

"Just like Henry David Thoreau!" I said cheerfully.

Like all the Transcendentalists, Thoreau was a great walker. He required at least four hours a day to maintain his physical and spiritual health; when he considered with a shudder the mechanics and shopkeepers who had to sit all day, he felt that they "deserve some credit for not having all committed suicide long ago."

What if this guy were the reincarnated ghost of Henry David Thoreau? I thought. And just like that, it was decided: I was chatting with Thoreau.

And of course, I wasn't. But what would be a more meaningful interaction: to tolerate this guy's presence and dismiss him? Or to view him, if not as the reincarnated ghost of my ultimate celebrity crush, then at least as a member of that ancient and honorable class of walkers?

"What made you stop traveling?" I asked.

"I got married…"

"Ahh. How old were you?"

"This was around when my son was born… and that was 1985, so… 32."

"Hey, that's when I was born! And I'm 32 now!"

The two kooks looked at each other, neither of them missing the significance of this moment. Here was a man who had exactly twice the life experience as I did. I felt like I'd been granted a glimpse at, if not my future, then at least one way the storyline might shake out.

Never stop walking, I reflected as I biked away. *But maybe also watch that you don't get too nutty.*

*

Jack and I regard each other warily. We're vaguely related, and we have the same haircut, but that's about all we have in common. For one thing, he's a child; I just feel like one.

"Do you want to hold him?" his father, my cousin Richard, asks.

"Uh, yeah!" I lie. My palms are sweating. Why am I so damn nervous?

In Chichewa, boy is mnyamata and man is amuna. You're not considered amuna until you've had a child. (The same goes for girls/atsikana and women/akazi.) It's a linguistic reflection of that great cross-cultural universal: Nothing makes you feel less like an adult than when someone your age has a baby. With the birth of Jack, Richard is officially an amuna. And as I nervously face the prospect of holding this uncertain-looking little human larva, I have never felt more like a mtsikana.

I remember in middle school, one of our teachers took maternity leave, and when she came back with the new baby, all the girls in my class clustered around her to fawn over it. I hung back at the edges of the pack. Why would I be interested in a bald, sticky, drooling lump that might shit itself at any moment?

That was pretty much my thinking on babies until my late 20s. I'd had it with bartending, so I got a job in a daycare instead. (It's basically the same, only the hours are better.) Conceptualizing babies as tiny, helplessly drunk people made them a lot less intimidating, and I even got to the point where I could grudgingly admit that some of them can sometimes be a little cute, sorta.

So why am I so nervous about holding this particular baby?

You'll change your mind. Women have a biological clock. Your priorities will change. What if, as soon as Jack is in my lap, some invisible switch flips, and everything I'm doing suddenly seems meaningless when compared to the prospect of growing a human inside me?

Jack looks almost as uneasy as I feel, his brow knit in a caricature of worry. But I'm not one to let my fears control me. I take a deep breath and settle him in my lap. Within a few moments, he determines that this tall, broad stranger is not a threat, and my uterus doesn't suddenly start demanding a sperm donation. Maybe there really is no such thing as a biological clock.

---

dear sara,

Thank you so much for getting your students involved with Represent the Village! I can't believe you guys raised $153 from a lemonade stand. Remember when we did that lemonade stand when we were kids… in a fire lane on a 45 mph road in rural Maine? I think we pulled in six bucks to split between the four of us.

But I digress. It also meant a lot that you believed in what I was doing, because there were times when *I* didn't even believe in what I was doing. And thanks for giving me a chance to speak to your kids! I liked how the only thing they cared about was the picture of the upside-down car.

"Why was that car in the woods??"

"How did it get in the woods?!"

"Why is it upside-down???"

"Does anyone have any questions about her *bike ride*?" you broke in.

I don't know if you remember, but this one kid asked, "Is it hard to ride your bike across the country?"

It's the most reasonable question in the world, and no adult would ever ask it. Who knew fifth graders could be so wise? I opened my mouth to answer, but then I thought about it for a second, and I laughed with delight. I think I said something like, "No, it's easy. You just ride a bike every day."

And although there's truth to that, it's not quite right. Because it's not easy to ride your bike across the country. It's really hard sometimes! Powering up mountains, going downhill in the stinging rain, carefully traversing a desert on a cloudless 95-degree day. It's hard to overcome the fear of camping out, and it can be hard to maintain conversations with the people who open their home to you. Even — especially? — family.

Is it hard to ride your bike across the country?

It was a question I'd reflect on for the rest of my trip.

Aunt Skeet is 90 years old and going strong. She's never had a surgery and takes minimal medication. She still does all her own cooking, cleaning, and gardening in a two-story house in New Hampshire. And she's always impeccably dressed, with a dozen silver bangles jingling on each delicate wrist.

"You are such an inspiration," I told her. "What's your secret?"

"A good man," she answered immediately and, raising her rocks glass, added, "and a good cocktail."

She lived with her partner Don for more than 50 years, but they never got married. As the decades wore on, their friends and family would ask, "Why don't you two just tie the knot already?" They'd share a smirk and respond, "We're waiting to see if we like each other."

I love their love story. They didn't have the ceremony or the piece of paper, the legal/religious/social substantiation of their relationship. They didn't need all that. They had each other.

He passed back in 2016 of Alzheimer's disease, and now she lives alone. She volunteers at the home where he spent his final weeks. She has cocktail hour with her friends, or over the phone with my grandmother in Florida. She carries his memory. Sometimes it's heavy, but it's never a burden, and that I think is love.

---

diner break: country cookin at the circle
(epson, n.h.)

It has the feel of a hotel banquet hall and everyone around you speaks with the papery refinement that is the accent of rural New Hampshire. You'll call your father, and he'll reminisce about an AM radio country music show that used to broadcast out of Epson. You will smile thinking about your father as a child, lying on the floor in front of the radio, tapping his toes and listening to the Epson Circle Country Show.

Rob is visiting family in New Hampshire, so he picks me up so we can go on a road trip to Montreal. As soon as we get in the car, I become mad with power.

"Rob, I get to choose the music."

"Okay." Rob has learned to be agreeable when I demand control of the stereo (even though he has literally the best taste in music in the world).

"It's Nahko and Medicine for the People. You have to love them."

"I love them!"

"No sass!" I yell. "Hey, I have a present for you." I hand him a plastic bracelet I found outside Kim's Kitchen.

"Why are you giving me a bracelet that says 'Liberty or Death'?"

"Because your *kyiiiiiin* is from New Hampshire. Hey Rob, say kin."

"Kin."

"No, say it like this: *kyiiiiiiiin*."

"Kyiiiiiiiiiiin."

I cackle. "My *kyiiiiiin* is from New Hampshire too. Live free or die!"

"Live free or die!"

"HEY ROB wanna play a game I just made up?

"Sure." Rob has learned to be agreeable when I propose games (even though they inevitably have no rules, no winners, and no point).

"It's called ROBROBROBROB. Here's how you play, are you ready?"

"Yes."

"ROBROBROBROBROBROBROBROB! Now it's *your* turn!"

"BROOKEBROO—"

"NO!"

"What?!"

"You're doing it wrong! It's called ROBROBROBROB not BROOKEBROOKEBROOKE! Now do it again!"

"ROBROBROBROBROBROBROBROBROB!!"

"I see you've played ROBROBROBROBROB before! Hey Rob!"

"Yes?"

"Wanna play a game I just made up?"

"Is it BROOKEBROOKEBROOKE?"

"HOW DID YOU KNOW?!"

"BROOKEBROOKEBROOKEBROOKE!"

"ROB, LOOK!"

Time slows and our jaws drop as we slide past a sign that says, I shit you not... **Brook Road**.

And that, dear friends, is how Rob Campbell became the world champion of BROOKEBROOKEBROOKE.

*

"Do you remember the time you came and gave me your college essays, and you had those blisters covering half your palms from transplanting rice?" I ask Freza.

"Yeah, I really do."

"Those are the gnarliest blisters I've ever seen. And I've hiked the Appalachian Trail."

Back in those days, Freza was a skinny teenager. He lived in a mud-brick house with a straw roof with his parents and seven younger siblings. His home village was a four-mile walk from Chikweo, the nearest place with electricity. He walked that road every day — even when he was hungry, even when he was sick, even when he was chased away from campus because he didn't have school fees — because he believed that education had the power to change his life.

And it did. The last time I saw him, I had just gotten out of the Peace Corps. I did a long Greyhound trip up the east coast to visit friends and family. We met at the library on McGill's MacDonald campus; it felt so good to hear a Malawian accent. It was February in Montréal, and the wind kicking up off the St.

Lawrence River was so harsh it made my eyes water, but he was wearing a windbreaker with the sleeves rolled up to his elbows.

"The door opens for you," he remarked as we walked out into the bitter cold. "Back home you had to open the door, but here it opens for you."

Compare him to the college senior sitting across from me, speaking effortless English. "Hard work" doesn't even begin to describe how this young man got from there to here.

"What advice would you give to Friday if he gets into an American university?" I ask him now.

"It will be the hardest thing you've ever done," he says.

"Harder than transplanting rice?"

He laughs and shakes his head. "A lot harder. I had no idea what I was getting into."

He talks about how in his freshman year, he felt hopelessly behind. He felt stupid. The amount of work he had to put in just to catch up to everyone else was daunting.

"I hear that," I say. "I had a 1.9 GPA after my first semester of college."

"Really?"

"Yeah." I shrug. "I was used to always being one of the smartest kids in my class without really having to try. But then when I got to college, it was a whole different world. All these other kids had private high school educations and tutors, all these resources I didn't even know *existed*, and I was so intimidated that I decided if I couldn't succeed, then I'd fail intentionally, and it would at least be my decision."

He looks confused; I'm not sure if it's the fuzzy logic or if he can't believe that the person who helped him apply to college almost flunked out herself. What can I say? To preserve my ego, I decided that *I* wasn't stupid, the *system* was stupid, and I was just too smart to go to class. And I still turned out okay in the end.

"That's why I admire you so much," I continue. "You came from a completely different world. You learned on a *chalkboard*. You could have given up, and no one would have faulted you, but instead you worked your ass off."

"Yes I did," he says. I feel a twinge of guilt. Who did I think I was, transplanting this kid, forcing him to struggle in this strange new environment?

"Was it worth it?" I ask.

Without a moment's hesitation: "Yes."

*

At dinner that night, I sliced into my burrito and jumped back at the rivulet of grease that spurted out. Cautiously, I nudged the flap of tortilla aside, revealing... a damp mound of corn kernels and limp onions.

"Oh my god," I said under my breath. "*Rob this is so bad.*"

He looked queasily at the crime scene that was his taco salad.

"I guess a restaurant called Casa Burrito in *rural Vermont* probably isn't the most authentic Mexican food," I whispered.

Rob laughed quietly. He has a great laugh — like the rheumatic wheezing of an old bus. "I don't know what this is," he whispered back, "but it's not Mexican food."

"*Rob it's just onions and corn!*"

We lurched in our seats with the force of suppressed laughter. Around us, civilized families celebrated Mother's Day, as our waitress flailed from table to table in a state of sheer panic[15].

---

[15] It was her first day ever working as a waitress. I recognized her immediately: awkward, vulnerable, earnest but naïve, maybe even clueless. She was me when I was that age.

To that waitress: Have you found the beauty in it yet? Have you tapped into that graceful dance, where your every movement has intention? Have you learned how to read people's minds in a glance? I hope you stick with it, girl, because waitressing is basically a superpower.

"It's like," I mused, pushing a pile of corn around my plate, "someone heard about Mexican food and thought, *I can make that!*"

"They heard about it from a grandmother who just had it for the first time!" Rob gasped.

"Or like from a book written in the 1800s!" I cackled.

"They overheard two people arguing about what Mexican food is and thought, *Now* there's *a restaurant idea!*"

My stomach protesting the massive amount of corn, onions, and grease I'd just consumed, Rob and I set out to find a place to stay. There was only one campground nearby. It was across the road from the Dollar General and cost $20 for a tent site.

"*Hell* no!" I hollered, smacking the dashboard. "This is my *homeland*. This is the most beautiful place in the world! This is *Vermont*, god dammit, and I am a *Vermonter*, and if you think I'm paying 20 bucks to pitch a tent in a field across the road from the Dollar General, you can go right back to *New Hampshire* where you belong!"

"Okay," Rob said. He's learned to be agreeable when I rant about Vermont.

I peered at the map and said, "What about Kill Kare?"

"Kill Kare?"

"Oh my god, it's actually Kamp Kill Kare."

"With three K's?"

"Of *course.*"

"That's regrettable," Rob chuckled.

Regrettable name notwithstanding, it's a lovely place: a swell of grass shaded with sugar maples and Lake Champlain nibbling at the pebbly beach. Especially on a summer night, with a warm wind stirring the water into gentle waves and an incandescent tiger lily sky. We sat together on a rock, Rob and I, and regarded this beauty in awed silence.

"This is a day use park," Rob observed. "I'm not sure we're allowed to camp here."

I didn't take my eyes off the sunset. "Live free or die, Rob."

*

I am Ms. Vermont. Got me a Vermont tattoo, wore a Vermont t-shirt on the Appalachian Trail, voted for Bernie Sanders in 2016. If you ever want to get me fired up, just say these magic words: "Vermont is upside-down New Hampshire."

The difference between New Hampshire and Vermont is the difference between Hillary Clinton and Bernie Sanders. Between Dr. Pepper and Moxie[16]. Between the green of a dollar bill and the green of a maple leaf.

Don't get me wrong; I love the gloomy splendor of New Hampshire. I spent my last day in the Granite State tracing a dirt bike path littered with dry orange pine needles. To my right, a periwinkle pond, trees with delicate green leaves straining from the tips of their branches, and a mysterious wooden sign that read, "One Long Whistle." I ran out of food and water climbing a 3,000-foot mountain, but a guy working on a house shared some water from a jug in his truck. Further on down the road, at Proctor's General Store, I sat on the front porch and ate one of the best meals of my life — a veggie wrap, a banana, string cheese, macaroni salad, and two cookies.

But crossing the bridge between Hanover, New Hampshire and Norwich, I felt something inside me relax. It's a deep tension, one I carry so constantly that I only notice it when it's gone.

Where's home?

The state of Vermont.

*

---

[16] Actually, Moxie is more of a Maine thing, but you can find it in Vermont too, if you know which country stores to check.

That night I stayed with a couple named Henry and Leigh. Henry was the principal of a school, and he gave me an insider's view into the American education system. We also talked about bike touring, and taking your time to appreciate the details.

"I admire your spirit and your pace," he said with a smile.

The next morning as I was leaving, their dog slipped past me and sprinted off into the woods. Leigh's shoulders slumped as she watched the dog running free-spiritedly around their property.

"Do you want me to try to help catch her?"

"It's futile," she sighed. "She'll come back when she feels like it."

"Bummer…"

"Eh, it means I get to go into work late."

In Vermont, the dogs are still wild.

*

I clawed my way up a steep, vicious little mountain with the rain dripping around me like a murmured conversation. As I shot downhill, that same rain pierced like shrapnel. When my momentum finally bled out, I was greeted by… another mountain and yet more rain.

The biker's life for me.

There was no waiting this storm out in a café (and believe me, I tried). So I accepted it. I would be wet and cold and tired. Bring it on.

I think people conflate acceptance with defeat. But how do you conquer the rain? If you stay inside, you're letting your fear of getting wet control you, and the rain *wins*. So accept and embrace it — like a moist, chilly hug from ol Mother Nature herself. I'll tell ya what, nothing makes you appreciate a warm shower and dry clothes quite like being wet and cold all day.

I also think the universe rewards gratitude. On the way up that last hill, I told the rain I appreciated it — at least I'm not hot! and hey, who needs water breaks when you can just turn your face up to the sky? — and when I got to the top, the clouds parted. With vibrant Vermont spread out before me, I coasted through warm sunshine all the way into Middlebury.

That night, I stayed with Bill and Ellen, old friends of the family who've known me since I was born. Ellen is a being of pure light and love, one of those rare humans who seems utterly at peace with herself, and who extends that peace to the people around her. Bill initially comes off as charmingly befuddled, but beyond his spectacles lays the gaze of a fine woodworker. He's a man fluent in the language of wood grain, who always measures twice. Their house is clean and cluttered in a way that invites you to throw off your coat and shoes and sit and chat awhile. And as soon as you do, their goof of a yellow lab, Charlie, will clamber straight in your lap. His thinking, as far as I could tell, is that since he wants to be in your lap, obviously that's what you want too.

See? he seems to say as he gazes adoringly up at you. *Everybody's happy!*

*

Biking along the next day, I thought: Haven't heard from Friday in awhile. I wonder what he thinks about all this... Malawians are so polite it can be hard to know what they're actually thinking. What would I do if Ms. Chaput decided to ride a bike across the country to help me apply to college? I'd be like... lady, what are you doing? That's so much work! What if I couldn't match her enthusiasm, those expectations?

No, this is different. Friday is Malawian; he grew up in a culture where it's a *thing* to have American volunteers move to your village. He specifically asked me for help.

But does he really even understand what this entails? Does he really, truly want to go to college in America? If he did, wouldn't he be contacting me more? I *know* he has what it takes, but does *he* believe that? Will the colleges believe that?

I keep hearing the same message from these admissions counselors: They wish they could let in students like Friday, but... and then they give me a look that says, "The money isn't there." And so they reject these students on the basis of SAT scores or GPA. Can Friday not be judged on his own merits? Can they really not recognize his tenacity, his potential? Are you saying you can't educate a hard-working, motivated student? If not, what kind of school are you? Are you a school at all, or just a business?

But also like... shouldn't *Friday* be the one saying this, not me?

I took a deep breath and sighed, and decided to include Friday more. Send him pictures of the schools, fun facts, reasons to get excited to start applying. If he tells me he doesn't want to apply, that's fine. He gets to make his own decisions. And my message still holds true.

*

As a kid, I always thought Route 17 led straight into a fairy tale. It takes you through one of those mountain forests that's always shaded, where the light glows in patches of green and gold, where it smells like ferns and living black soil. A perfectly plausible habitat for leprechauns and fairies. There's an A-frame where the road bends sharply to the left. A house... shaped like a TRIANGLE? It may as well have been an enchanted castle to my little kid brain.

And the names of the places you pass! Jerusalem, Buel's Gore, Mad River Glen. This kingdom has a kind of beauty with hidden power and sharp teeth. Like a lynx.

... wait a second, Mad River Glen? I'm not going that direction.

Oh no.

I pulled over and, wincing, looked at my phone.

Sure enough, Mapsy had crashed. I had just biked up a damn mountain for no reason.

"FFFFFFFFFFFFFUUUUUUUUUUCK!!!!"

That's the nice thing about being in the middle of an enchanted forest. Nobody but the leprechauns and fairies can hear you scream.

And then I tried to laugh it off. *At least you get to go downhill now*, I told myself. But I was still pissed off. I shot so much energy on this stupid mistake.

Even in my bad mood, I had to concede that the ride downhill was exhilarating — clean, smooth blacktop rising and dipping like gentle moguls through green fields dotted with dandelions. I can say, without a trace of bias, that Vermont in the summertime is the most beautiful place in the world.

And then, up ahead, I saw a woman with a bike turned upside down.

"Need a hand?"

"If you can, that would be wonderful. I put my sweatshirt on the back rack and it got caught in the brake."

It was an easy fix: I used an Allen wrench to loosen the brake, freed the scrap of fabric, and then tightened everything back up. The woman introduced herself as Bradlee and told me a bit about her life.

She was trying to get back into biking,

you know,

to get some direction.

Her life was somewhat turbulent at the moment—

her husband of 20 years had just asked for a divorce.

Her kids were grown;

maybe she could move to Massachusetts,

but Vermont was her home;

and I guess —
it's just a scary thing to have to start over
in your 40s.

And then she looked at me like I was a magical fairy sent to her by the universe, and asked, "What should I do?"

She reminded me of my mom, and how she must have felt after she divorced my dad, trying to learn how to do right for herself after years of living under someone else's rules. What if my mom met a mysterious stranger at that point in her life? What would I want that stranger to tell her?

"I'm excited for you," I said. "You're free. And freedom is beautiful, but it's scary, because it's a blank page. The best thing I can think is to fill that page up with all the things you love."

The smile on Bradlee's face told me I was on the right track, so I forged ahead:

"My parents had a messy divorce. But a few years later, my mom met the love of her life. It makes me wonder, what if everything happens for a reason? Maybe you just have to trust that you have to go through the bad to get to the good. It might suck, but it's temporary. And the good news is, you're a woman, and you and I both know, there's nothing stronger than a woman."

I pedaled away smiling. If I hadn't gotten lost on that mountain, I never would have met Bradlee. *See?* I told myself. *Trust the setbacks and love the discouraging times. It's all part of the current that's taking you where you're meant to be.*

*

My dad built his own house in the woods. Upstairs is his wife's domain. Natural light spills through tall windows, catching the flecks of gold in the black granite countertops. There's modern bamboo flooring on one side, more black granite on the other, a stone chimney and a top-of-the-line pellet-burning woodstove. Upstairs it's all smooth-sanded wood and precise 90-degree angles. Upstairs is a love letter to his wife.

Down the wrought-iron spiral staircase — careful, it wobbles — to my father's basement. It's where he started, where he made the mistakes he didn't repeat upstairs. He persuaded his friends to come help him with 24-packs of Genesee Cream Ale, so some of the doorknobs turn backward and the bathroom door doesn't close all the way. An old-fashioned woodstove with a cast-iron kettle, an upright piano; two mismatched chairs pulled up to a table strewn with:

- old envelopes with notes on the back in neat cursive written so hard it indents the paper
- a stub of a pencil, no eraser, sharpened with
- a pocketknife
- a deck of cards worn soft at the edges
- a cribbage board in the shape of Vermont
- a harmonica (key of D) in a scuffed case
- an AM/FM radio
- books: a guide to hiking trails in Vermont, a novel by Haruki Murakami
- a red coffee cup with a picture of Lenin's face
- a Heineken tallboy

My dad's house is a mirror, a reflection of his nature: deliberate but eccentric, a kind of accidental poetry. It's not dissimilar from this trip I'm on, this mission I'm trying to accomplish. Well-meaning and carefully planned, but not without its flaws. Like father like daughter, I suppose.

*

SLOW
CAUTION
TURTLE
CROSS
ING!!!!!

read the hand-painted sign. It was so clumsy and sincere only a child could have made it.

What happens during the transition to adulthood that makes a person believe that getting where they're going is more important than the life of a turtle? Why aren't more adults outraged about what's happening to the planet? How is environmentalism considered a matter of *opinion*?

The breeze ruffled my dress and the surface of the water, and I imagined the turtles swimming there, safe thanks to the efforts of this brave little sign. Sunlight sifted through the choppy air to settle on my shoulders and the Adirondacks alike.

We have mistaken our ideas for reality, I thought, gazing across the lake. *This is reality.*

*

I called the Beekmantown Fire Department and asked if I could camp there.

"I'm afraid we can't give you permission," she told me sternly. "And there's no one on duty."

Sounds like a yes to me.

---

diner break: guma's diner (west chazy, n.y.)

Pancakes so big and fluffy they could double as seat cushions.

I spent a soggy couple of days pushing through a constant cold drizzle. All my clothes were damp. My rain shell was saturated; it clung uselessly to my puffy jacket, but I didn't dare take it off. There was a big muddy stripe running right down the center of my butt from all the road water my back wheel was throwing up, and I couldn't get warm. The world was slick asphalt and young leaves trembling beneath gloomy, steel-colored clouds.

I'd scrape out a hard 10 or 15 miles and then pay for a place to sit and try to warm up. I drank hot water out of a Styrofoam cup in a shitty pizza joint and looked out the window, my shoulders slumped with disappointment.

I managed another 12 miles that day. When I spied a muddy four-wheeler trail blocked by a fallen tree, it looked like home. I stashed my bike out of sight of the road and pitched my tent under some skinny trees. As soon as I got into my little shelter, I felt a fierce wave of self-sufficiency. The price of freedom is riding in the rain, but in this bleak, lonely, rainy world, I had found a dry place to sleep.

---

diner break: leonard's cherry-knoll restaurant (burke, n.y.)

Rain running down a plate-glass window seems almost like a living thing. A troop of worms wriggling busily downward, hesitating and changing direction, leaving trails and deltas and islands scattered in their wake. How nice it is, to wake up in the mud, ride a cold few miles, and end up in a warm diner with ruffled periwinkle curtains and booths with squishy cushions, watching the rain find its meandering way from the clouds to the earth.

On my way out, I paused at a world map in the entranceway, with clusters of pins marking the patrons' hometowns. There, in the Malawian capital of Lilongwe, was a lone pin. There's never a pin in Malawi.

I took three pins and put them in Fairfield, Chikweo, and McMurdo. These tough, beautiful little places I've been lucky enough to call home.

What is freedom?

Lounging on a limestone ledge on the side of US 11, smoking a joint, and watching the cars roll by.

"The Computer Dog," read the cardboard lawn sign, and I laughed. What a weird concept for a small business! Like... maybe this guy has a dog, and it's the mascot for his computer-fixing side hustle?

Upon closer inspection, it actually said, "The Computer Doc." *How funny*, I thought. *You switch one letter, and the entire meaning changes.*

So naturally I went through the entire alphabet. Highlights:

- the computer fog (it's a virus)
- the computer hog (he keeps all the computers that come in)
- the computer hug (for when your computer's feeling down)
- the computer dom (for when your computer's feeling horny)
- the computer dot (uh, I believe the term is "pixel")

Computer dox, that's malaria medicine for your computer. Computer doy, a holdover from the '90s, like, computer doy, you don't know what's wrong with your computer? Computer doz... puts your computer right to sleep.

Then I glanced up and thought, *Hey, a lake!*

With nothing but time on your hands, a bike tour is the perfect opportunity to clean out the attic of your mind. You can ruminate on the entirety of your childhood and concoct every possible variation of your future, all before you get to Connecticut. Or to lunchtime!

Then you can make a list of every person you've ever slept with. You can try to count how many planes you've ridden in your life. Or maybe try to remember all the classes you took in college, and one thing you learned in each of them. Imagine what you'd say at a toast at your sister's wedding. Think about bananas. Have you ever *really* thought about bananas? Bananas are friggin weird!

Can you make a list of drugs for every letter of the alphabet? Acid, barbiturates, cocaine, DMT, ecstasy... What about derogatory terms for men? Asshole, bastard, cuckold... Sexual maneuvers? Autoerotic asphyxiation, bondage, cunnilingus, doggy-style...

Is it "doggy style" or "doggy-style"? Or "doggystyle?" No, that's preposterous. But if it were, that's... seven consonants in a row! Wow! Wait, no, "y" would be a vowel in that case. Hmm. What are some words with a lot of consonants in a row? *Switchblade... thoughtcrime... jockstrap, hah... borscht, strengths*[17], *catchphrase*[18]...

You listen to BBC News for a while because you're pretty sure you can feel yourself getting dumber. There's a story about the ongoing cholera outbreak in Yemen. You ponder the unfairness of proxy wars in the Middle East. It gets sad, so you imagine that you're the president. Now *you're* calling the shots! First order of business: Invite all world leaders into the Oval Office. Put a bunch of squishy cushions on the floor, drape the walls with velvet tapestries, and burn some sandalwood incense. Play *Magical Mystery Tour* or *Abbey Road*, something everyone can agree is awesome. Then pull out the biggest blunt in the world and pass it around until everyone decides to be friends.

PRESIDENT MARSHALL STRIKES GLOBAL PEACE ACCORD IN SINGLE PLEASANT AFTERNOON

---

[17] This one was a contribution by my sister's brilliant friend Andrew. He writes *New York Times* crossword puzzles and played this game with me, no questions asked, when I texted him from the side of the road.

[18] Also Andrew's, after a triple-text about how strangely enough, he had just been mulling the transliteration of the Russian character щ. Also, he dropped "sequoia" on me and my brain exploded. Some people don't need bike tours to go down grammatical rabbit holes.

the headlines scream.

MARSHALL, OTHER WORLD LEADERS, DEVISE PLAN TO SPREAD "GOOD VIBES WORLDWIDE"

Together with all your new friends, you climb Mount St. Helens and dump a bunch of psilocybin mushrooms in its mouth, then tickle that sucker til it erupts. Humanity collectively comes to the conclusion that if everybody were just chill and nice, it would solve all the problems we have the power to solve.

You look down at your phone. You still have like 12 miles to go.

Ithaca, N.Y.
50 days · 1,990 miles

The timeline for the last few years of my life goes like this:

Grad school/drove an 18-wheeler > Peace Corps Malawi > Appalachian Trail > waitressed in Ithaca for a bit > Alaska > Antarctica > cross-country bike tour

One of these things is not like the others.

The thing is, even though it's not as impressive as the Peace Corps or the AT, Ithaca was an important chapter in my life. I lived with my sister, and we got to connect as adults and peers. I`discovered yoga and rock climbing, learned how to save money, and got in touch with my spiritual side. It was the perfect place to reacclimatize to American culture after two and a half years in the village and six months in the woods. I think my sister invited me to live with her because she secretly thought I'd like Ithaca enough to put down roots. She wasn't wrong; if I were going to live anywhere, a small, liberal city surrounded by great hiking and biking and only a few hours' bus ride to New York City would probably be it.

But I was born to ramble. That was something else I learned in Ithaca.

It was good to come back, but I was a little nervous too. Ithaca had been a time of intense spiritual growth, but in Alaska, I regressed. I gained 20 pounds, abandoned my yoga practice, and spent the summer sullen, stoned, and alone. Antarctica and the bike tour had been healing so far, but returning to Ithaca was like backing up to a doorjamb where my height had been marked years ago. How would I measure up?

*

Cornell overlooks the rest of Ithaca from the lofty summit of a 900-foot hill. The most notorious way there is up East Buffalo Street. In the wintertime, slipping and falling on the icy 10.6-19.9% grade is a rite of passage. You're not a true Ithacan, it is said, until you've busted your ass on East Buffalo.

A less brutal route is University Ave., which winds around the hill at a comparatively gentle 5% grade. I know it well; it was my preferred bike route to the rock gym. Back then, all I had was a single-speed, and the last pitch always stopped me in my tracks. I'd have to get off and push to the top, red-faced with exertion and disgrace.

But not this time! Lucky and I crested the summit and I punched the air in victory. Turns out all you need to conquer University Ave. is a 1,500-mile running start.

Through the haze of endorphins, I had a rollicking conversation with Martin, a jovial admissions counselor with a big laugh.

"Malawi, Malawi," he said thoughtfully. "I know we had a student from Malawi a few years ago… She lives in the capital city now, doing work with EducationUSA —"

"Oh! Faith!"

"Yes!"

"Duh, I totally forgot she went here. I worked closely with her when I was in the Peace Corps. She's such a great person, isn't she?"

"Oh, I loved Faith. I still talk to her. What a small world."

"I know! Would you believe this isn't the first time I've been in one of these meetings and found out we knew someone in common?"

"You don't say!"

"I *do* say," I grinned. "See, this is why it's so important to educate students from diverse backgrounds. Faith is using the education she received to give back to her community. Cornell's investment in Faith pays dividends with every cohort of Malawian students who get accepted to American universities."

"I couldn't agree more."

We chatted like that for a couple hours, about development and education, about Africa's potential, but also about low-sugar diets and Ithaca culture. Graduation time is a lull for admissions counselors; the hardest part of their job is over, recruiting season isn't in full swing yet, and they can take a couple hours to have a conversation with an interesting traveler. I left feeling like I'd spent a fun few hours with an old friend. And then I had the distinct pleasure of barreling down East Buffalo. What goes up, after all, must come down.

The next day, my family and I and a few hundred others gathered in a gym and listened to a long list of names — people so curious about one specific thing that they spent the better part of a decade learning about it, researching it, and adding their humble handful of soil to the mountain of human knowledge.

One by one, the Ph.D.s walked across the stage in red robes and puffy hats. They seemed dazed, like they'd just woken up from a dream... or maybe like they hadn't slept in seven years. Did I detect a note of unease? Of adjusting to the fact that they had just undergone a fundamental redefinition of their identity, from student to doctor?

They called my sister's name — "Jillian Marshall, ethnomusicology" — and I cheered like a wild creature. You think riding a bike across the country is a long journey? Try seven years in a Ph.D. program.

At Jill's graduation party that night, I drank sparkling water with our dramaturge friend Anne. She's sweet and talented and a shrewd judge of character; if she were alive during the Salem Witch Trials, she would 100% have been burned at the stake. And then we sat in a circle with the new Ph.D.s and played a game they called "What's the Most Awkward Food to Bring to a Colloquium?" (The winners were a whole coconut, a box of uncooked pasta, and a single piece of sushi.)

There, feeling at home among my friends and family, I thought about how nervous I'd been on my way to Ithaca. *Would I measure up?* I'd wondered. The answer was, I hadn't grown or shrunk; I'd branched out. If I wouldn't expect a tree to grow in a straight line, why would I expect it from myself?

---

diner break: café dewitt (ithaca, n.y.)

I had a month-long case of creative block the first time I crept into Café DeWitt and slid into a corner seat, over where the two long fishtanks meet. The only other customer was a homeless guy sipping a cup of coffee at the counter. I took out a notebook of sketches from the Appalachian Trail and started inking them. The server — Lennon specs, corkscrew curls, red khaki pants rolled to the ankle — gave me an inquisitive look and kept the coffee coming. Time flew in a way it hadn't in weeks, and after two hours I'd finished several pages. With that, the creative block had lifted.

Two or three times a week, I'd sit in that same spot, drink endless coffee, and draw comics. If I wanted a treat, I'd pick at a fruit cup — the fruit cups at Café DeWitt are works of art, like a Kandinsky painting compressed into a ceramic mug. If I wanted a break, I'd chat with the servers, especially Tony and Sophie and Lucas with the Lennon specs. Sometimes I'd peek up at the other patrons eating brunch, and I'd wonder if they knew just how special this place really was.

Town Days are intoxicating. You have a place to sleep! You don't have to carry all your stuff around! Are you going to the post office? How exotic! How... quotidian!

I love that word, *quotidian*. I think it must have been coined by an adventurer, because only someone whose life is completely unpredictable would use a beautiful word like "quotidian" to mean "mundane." But I got back on my bike, because I also love the word *bike*.

---

snapshots: leaving ithaca

That tangled field where one afternoon I laid on the damp grass and watched the clouds drifting back toward Ithaca. I was in love. Before that day, I wasn't sure if I would ever be in love again.

That thrift store in Trumansburg where I bought clothes four days after I finished the Appalachian Trail. I only owned one change of clothes. On the AT, that was enough, but like it or not, I was in the real world now.

That abandoned mental institution where Sherman and I went on our third date! Our first date was waffles and a four-mile hike. Our second date was car camping in the Adirondacks to take pictures of waterfalls in the snow. Things fizzled out when the relationship got to the let's-order-takeout-and-watch-a-movie phase. Maybe I'm high maintenance in my own way.

But gradually I passed the boundaries of my old world and back into the unknown. There were no reminders here, just me in my purest state, and the freedom to learn new things about myself.

Maybe one of these days I'll finally figure out who I am!

*

What is freedom?
Skipping stones on a beach while everyone else is at work.

*

I leaned under a birch tree in someone's front yard. I had no home, so the world was my home. And in that moment, my home was rolling farmland and beech forests, the glittering surface of Seneca Lake, and a cascade of spade-shaped leaves overhead, serrate edges rimmed in golden sunlight.

If gold is valuable because it's rare, than what about this?

*

Along Seneca Lake, I stopped to write in my journal:

Bike trail next to a lake,
the air is thick w/
honeysuckle.
paradise?

*

In Trumansburg, a man strolled toward me. His clothes and skin were the same leathery shade of brown, his hair was sun-streaked, and he was singing. He beamed at me; I gave him a polite smile/shrug/look-at-the-ground and kept walking.

A block or so later, I met his bike. It was a beat-up ugly old alleycat the color of swamp mud with a 20-gallon blue storage container bungeed onto a rack made out of plywood. It looked heavy and tough and strong. Suddenly, I understood. This man's wasn't crazy, he was just free. An honest-to-god human, same as me.

*

I caught sight of a brown blur tumbling along the double yellow line. I squinted, cocked my head. *What is that?* The realization hit, and I let out a wordless wail of despair.

It was a fawn, all alone, frantically running down the middle of State Route 148. As fragile as a matchstick lean-to. I've never seen anything so helpless.

She craned her neck to face me wild-eyed and darted into some bushes. I did a u-turn to follow her, but she was gone. And what could I do anyway? I guess the only thing you can do in that situation is pray:

uh hey uh the-universe-or-whatever, could you please keep an eye on that fawn? please make her mom be okay or a nice farmer adopts her or something, okay? thanks. i love you.

That's how I pray, I dunno how you do it.

*

On a paved path along a lake with the sun slipping down, I passed two women walking hand-in-hand.

"How does it feel for you?" one asked.

"Natural," the other responded. "Like it's sposta be happening."

I leaned Lucky against a bench and sat to watch the sunset. The sky was a puddle of melted sherbet, and the water puckered in reverse, like rain was falling up from the depths of the lake. Fish eating the bugs that hovered over the water in a thin fog. I breathed in the warm, turmeric-tinted air. My only companion was a heron on a far-away rock.

Is it hard to ride your bike across the country?

No, it's *easy!*

The next morning, I was unlocking my bike when a guy walked up and asked, "Goin far?"

"Cross the country."

He reminded me of a matchstick: tall and skinny, with a red face. "Why?" he asked with an expectant smile.

"It seemed like fun!"

"No, I mean… *why*?"

I paused, a little puzzled, then lit up. "I'm raising money for Malawian college students, and awareness about—"

He held up his right hand and reached into his pocket with his left. "That's what I was lookin for. Here ya go."

He pulled out his wallet, handed me five bucks, and walked away.

Greece Canal Park, Rochester, N.Y.
58 days · 2,196 miles

Beneath the wan remnants of a pancake-batter sunset, in a patch of woods behind a little league field in Greece Canal Park, our intrepid heroine pushes her bike along a muddy trail and through a miasma of mosquitoes. She has long since given up the dream of an Instagram campsite; like a lonely barfly at last call, she'll take what she can get.

I find a reasonably flat spot and lean Lucky against a tree. Time to kick back and relax. And by that I mean… laboriously construct my shelter for the evening! After laying the ground cloth, staking the tent, feeding the poles through the guides, strapping on the rainfly, locking up my bike, inflating my sleeping pad, laying out my sleeping bag, brushing my teeth, changing out of my bike shorts, and killing all the mosquitoes[19] that had gotten into my tent, I finally lay down… and there's a pointy rock digging into my spine.

But it's dark, and I don't feel like undoing all my hard work and shifting it two inches to the left only to find a root poking me in the kidney and 20 more mosquitoes in my tent. This, I

---

[19] I normally try not to kill bugs, but these guys had it coming.

141

decide, is an opportunity to practice acceptance. (In other words, I say "fuck it.")

I watch an episode of "Breaking Bad" on my phone — because there's nothing like watching an hour of gratuitous violence[20] to help a gal unwind after a 60-mile bike ride. I fall into a restless sleep…

…and wake up at 2 a.m. to the sound of a dentist's drill outside my tent.

My eyes pop open. Silence. What was that noise? Maybe it was just a —

Rhnnnnnnnnn!

Whatever it is, it's getting closer. I turn on my flashlight, and the serial killer bounds crashingly through the underbrush.

I lay there, barely breathing, frozen and alert, adrenaline coursing through my veins.

Fiddlehead pipes up: *what if there's someone crazy outside my tent who wants to hurt me?*

There isn't, Maple says firmly. *I'm sure it's just an animal, and I don't think there are bears around here, so we're good.*

And then a third, unfamiliar voice: *If you had let a guy come with you on this trip, he could be handling this right now.*

RHNNNNNNNN!

Ahh fuck.

I get out of my tent, wave my flashlight around, and yell, "I MEAN YOU NO HARM. JUST LET ME SLEEP!" I bend down and grope around until I find a big stick, and then spear it into the muddy ground outside my tent. To use as a weapon, I guess?

RNNNNNNNNN!

Okay, now this is just annoying. "GO *AWAY!*" I yell, and then under my breath: "God, take a hint!"

---

[20] For those who've seen the show, it was "Negro y Azul," with Danny Trejo and the tortoise.

Silence. I think we're okay. I crawl back into my tent, now filled with mosquitoes, and text my dad. I try to relax, but my brain is caught in a tug-of-war between Sleep and Fear. Every time it looks like Sleep is going to win, Fear jerks the rope, and my eyes pop open.

The next morning, I emerge from my tent smeared with mud, dead mosquitoes, and my own blood, and a text from Dad explaining that, "deer make all kinds of noises."

*

After three days and 200 miles without a shower, I raced thunderstorms and a caffeine crash to Niagara Falls and won. The night before, I was a homeless vagrant facing off against a wild animal at 2 a.m. Today, I was just another tourist.

I almost didn't make it. The bike path was a race outta hell, and I followed blind instinct along the surface streets of Niagara Falls. No time to dawdle and check the map — the hostel check-in closed at 7, and at the rate I was going, I was going to make it there at 6:58.

The hostel owner greeted me with crossed arms and a scowl. He seemed like the type who would NOT have let me check in at 7:01. The type who looks at the world as if it were trying to impress him, and failing.

But it didn't matter, because here I was at Niagara Falls. A place I had wanted to visit for... well, all of five hours. Just a funny way to motivate myself to do some miles. Even though I grew up in the Northeast, this was a tourist attraction that had managed to escape me. Turns out to see it, I had to bike all the way from south of the Mason-Dixon line.

I navigated the circus of tacky attractions and followed a path that deposited me upriver of the falls. The water rushed like a crowd flowing into a concert venue, pulled by the insistence of gravity, tumbling and crashing into rocks. The air vibrated with the sound of rushing water. The sheer kinetic energy was infectious; I walked fast like I was trying to catch a plane.

Overhead, a cloudbank like a thick comforter pulled halfway over an incandescent orange sky. I walked amidst tourists speaking Hindi, Mandarin, English, Spanish, French, German, beneath the sublime surrealist painting overhead. In my excitement, I loved each and every one of them. We were all sharing this enchanted moment, creating it in our overlapping consciousness.

And then I saw it —

the precipitous drop.

Precipitous is really the only word to describe it. 635,000 gallons per *second* spilling down a chasm the height of the Arc de Triomphe. Did people really go over this in barrels? I loved them too. There in the air suffused with saffron, I loved the falls and everyone around me and the power and majesty of this moment. The flashing neon lights, the tacky tourist traps — they were endearing in their insignificance compared to this, the very presence of god. Like a mosquito biting the Buddha.

How entirely human, I thought. *How charmingly, quixotically human.* Making money on the banks of creation. Imagine how this place must have looked before. "WE WERE HERE TOO!" those neon lights screamed. I pitied them, for missing the point, but I forgave them too. My ego consumed in the crashing power of water.

*

When I was a kid, my mom used to wake up hours before everyone else to sketch at the dining room table, this great round slanted hunk of wood with legs that ended in lion paws. We'd find her hunched over the table, drinking coffee (2% milk and Sweet'n Low), with the red-and-white deer blanket draped over her shoulders, working on some minute detail in a drawing of a house. A brick, a stone in the walkway, a

144

windowpane: The manmade elements were always painstakingly detailed, but the plants were carefree smudges.

And my dad. Boots squeaking in the snow through the frozen darkness of a pre-dawn Vermont winter morn that swallows and dulls the edges of the roaring dragon that is his truck. Harmonicas and construction plans scattered across the dashboard, dry heat spilling from dusty vents, a jug of half-frozen spring water at my feet. Coffee hot off the percolator steaming like a genie from a plastic mug; Camel cigarettes; the crackle of AM radio. My father wedges himself behind the wheel and puts the truck in gear.

As a kid, I didn't understand why my parents liked the morning. It felt awful to be awake that early, like drowning in brownie batter. But I get it now. It's a sacred time of day. Pure potential. Anything could happen. Why, it could even be the greatest day of your life.

I leave the hostel early, and follow my front wheel for one last look at Niagara. There is no sound beyond the whirring of my bike tires, the silver notes of birdsong, and the continual rumble of the falls. An occasional car passes, its taillights like burning garnets. I give them a soft smile of recognition, maybe a little wave. We're members of an exclusive club, after all: We're crepuscular.

The falls are no less majestic in the light of the sunrise, with just a few scattered tourists, early birds like me. I stand and drink them in again. "Love Letters to God" is pleasantly stuck in my head.

Love letters to god / I wonder if she reads them / or if they get lost / in the stars / the stars / in the stars

Upriver, there are signs explicitly forbidding people from entering the water. On principle, I walk past them and dip my feet in. My humble feet, which have touched so much earth and carried me so far. I feel connected to this river, this great mother.

Morning's sacred stillness lasts until it ends, and then the world begins to stir and stretch and wiggle its fingers and toes. Heading west, the sunrise is behind me, so I read it secondhand: the sky gradually lightening to violet to baby blue to pallid white and eventually back again to the hale and hearty cerulean of daytime. This is the time of day when the cars appear, the cavalry of people going to work. I don't smile and wave at them. I feel self-conscious, like a child playing a game while the adults are irritated that they have to go to work, choking on brownie batter, so I stay out of their way. Instead, I share a smile with the new infant day.

"It happens this way," I think. "Don't take it personally. They don't know how special you are. They don't know that today could be the greatest day of their life."

*

And the award for worst drivers in America goes to... Buffalo! Congratulations, Buffalo. Do you have a few words? Perhaps you could share the secret to your success?

"What an unexpected honor! Well you know, the secret is that our drivers have an *open animosity* toward cyclists. Not the outta-my-way rudeness of Baltimore, not the distracted indifference of Bostonians. We simply view bikers as a nuisance, and we use intimidation to drive them out of our city — pun *intended*!"

The cars were hostile, but the people were nice. I rested on a bench on the side of a river, among the folks with fishing poles sitting on lawn chairs and coolers. Two guys eyed me from a distance. They had tattoos beneath their eyes and every conceivable facial piercing. I returned their gaze, gave a little smile, and they rose and swaggered up to me, brandishing... a smallmouth bass.

146

"Do you want this fish?"

*

In the early morning, the day is pure potential. But as the sun rises and dries up the dew and bakes the hills around you, it begins to take form. Often, it's not the greatest day of your life. You might get lost, drivers might be rude, it might be cold, your ass might hurt. (Ain't that just the worst? It's bad enough to be in pain without the indignity of it being your ass.) Of course, your shoulders also hurt. Your spine is stiff, from your sacrum to your skull.

It's okay if you have to sit somewhere and sigh or cry or curse. Phone a friend, someone you trust enough to complain. My friend Mr. Tamani always used to say, "A problem shared is half-solved."

But every gravel driveway has a few pretty stones.

You might see a nice view, or sunlight illuminating the leaves of a tree overhead. You might have a funny interaction with another person. Some thuggy-looking guys might offer you a smallmouth bass. Your favorite song, a satisfying cup of coffee, a tacky statue of a dinosaur, the feeling of triumph of climbing a hill, bombing downhill, spotting a heron, taking a good picture, yelling out into the nothingness because you can, successfully peeing on the side of the road without being seen. If you look for the good, you'll find it.

Midday never lasts forever. The sun slides downward, the light deepens to gold, the sky ceases to burn, the shadows lengthen. I like to see the cars coming home from work. I hope the people driving them have something nice to look forward to. Someone they love, or a good meal. Maybe a bike ride? It makes me happy to see the people, finally free.

That night, I camped on a little bluff in a park overlooking Lake Erie. Not the stealthiest spot, but no one bothered me. There were four little kids playing in the water below, and one

147

of them yelled up at me, "You wanna come down and feel the water??"

"Is it warm?"

"No, it's COOOOOOOOLD!"

"I'll pass," I laughed.

The sky was muted sapphire, the water was wrinkled silk, the waves were rhythmic as a heartbeat. I scrunched my bare toes in the dirt, allowing a few mosquitos to bite me, because mosquitoes gotta eat too. Did you know it's only female mosquitoes that bite? They need blood to produce eggs. Thinking about mosquitoes as fellow ladies dealing with their pain-in-the-ass reproductive systems makes me like them a lot better.

So it wasn't the greatest day of your life.

Or hell, maybe it was.

Because it was a day in your life. And that's all our life is, is days. And just because one happened to have a little more happiness or a little more screaming curses in it than the others doesn't make it better or worse. You were alive.

Maybe when you die, you miss the feeling of mosquito bites, and sunburn, and thirst. I bet you remember the hard times fondly, and fonder still the relief that follows. I bet you miss the feeling of air in your lungs.

How lucky we are, to breathe.

These were my thoughts as I gazed at the sunset smooth and pink as the inside of a conch shell until the nighttime swallowed it up. Stars like Christmas lights, stars like mica, stars like trumpets, stars like swans. Safe in the world's great shadow, it's time to sleep, because tomorrow is a new day. As your dreams wrap long fingers around your mind, a tiny star comes to light inside you, burning with the excitement that you're only one sleep away from the next morning, and that sacred quiet, that seed of potential, that today could just be the greatest day of your life.

*

The next day, I was biking along when a truck slowed to match my pace. The window rolled down, and the guy driving hollered, "How far are you going??"

"All the way, baby!"

"Congratulations! I've been cross-country four times!"

"Good on ya!"

And then, with a thumbs-up and a big grin, he yelled, "Good luck, buddy!" and drove away. I had a laugh. Not enough people call women "buddy."

My thoughts began to wander, and they landed on Tawonga.

---

dear tawonga,

You are, without a doubt, one of the most important people who has ever passed through my life. You wouldn't be where you are today — pursuing a bachelor's at Earth University — if I hadn't essentially forced you to apply to the African Leadership Academy. And I wouldn't be on this quest to help more African students attain the education they deserve if it weren't for the success I had with you and Freza. We each changed each other's lives so profoundly that I have no idea how to have a relationship with you.

We're not friends. I was never technically your teacher, or even a mentor, really. (My role was so minimal: I just nominated you, typed up your application, and helped you get your visa.) I was your Peace Corps Volunteer. What a strange relationship.

When I try to talk to you, I feel awkward and wooden, hopelessly out of touch, like an absentee father making his monthly phone call to his ever-more-distant children. At the same time, I genuinely care about your life. I'm rooting for you. No matter what, no matter where you are, please know that I will always be sitting there in the stands with a big foam finger that says "TAWONGA #1" yelling, "You can do it! I believe in you!"

… As if you even need my encouragement. You're one of those people who's destined for greatness. And even though helping you and Freza is the thing I'm the most proud of in my life, I have to be careful, because you, Freza, and Friday are your own people, not my accomplishments.

North East, Penn.
60 days · 2,305 miles

The first thing I saw when I pulled up to Wayne's house was a Hummer with a Trump 2020 bumper sticker. It seemed I was going to have to do the unthinkable and — gasp! — *talk to someone with different political beliefs.* Fortunately, I've developed a strategy for exactly this sort of situation: Be their friend. Friendship starts with common ground, which in our case was alcohol and ghosts.

"Do you believe in ghosts?" I demanded.

He laughed. "Not really."

"Wait — *no* or *not really*?"

"Well…"

"WAYNE DID YOU SEE A GHOST?"

"… I'm a logical man. I'm analytical. I need the facts."

"Dude, of course. Everyone knows ghosts aren't real." I paused to take a long sip of the anise wine. "Oh my *god* Wayne, did you really *make* this?"

"I did!"

"This is the most delicious wine in the universe."

"You think so?"

I nodded. "Where was I?"

"Logically, we know that ghosts aren't real."

"*Exactly*. But there *are* things in life that we can't explain."

"I'll give you that."

"So with that being said... dude, my house growing up was *totally* haunted." And then I launched into my favorite ghost story:

Mom and Dad were off doing barn chores, and Jill and I were deep in a game of Crash Test Dummies, which largely consisted of running face-first into the wall. We were gearing up for another round when we heard the unmistakable sound of plates shattering in the kitchen. A shelf must have given out. We both looked at each other — *we both heard it* — and then wordlessly ran to the kitchen.

Not a dish out of place.

"That's a good one!" said Wayne. His cat Lea, half-blind with a snaggle tooth, jumped up in his lap.

"So even though we're both rational adults and we know they're totally not real... have you ever seen a ghost?" I asked. "Besides this bottle of wine, I mean?"

"Wanna open another?"

"*Do* I?!"

After perusing the bottles in his cellar, I decided on the cherry-rhubarb. And then he told me his tale:

He was in the bathroom at work. It was small, just a urinal and a single stall, so he checked under the partition to make sure he wasn't interrupting someone taking a dump. Coast clear.

"So I start doing my thing, and then I hear a grunting noise in the toilet stall like someone's taking a shit."

He figured whoever was in there must have had their feet up... but when he glanced through the crack in the partition, the stall was *empty*.

"DID YOU RUN AWAY??"

"No, but I'm just sorta confused, you know? I wasn't scared, I was just baffled. And then, while I had soap on my hands, I heard clearly the rustling of a newspaper."

"WHAT."

"I ran out of the bathroom, and I never went in again. Six months later, I found out that a guy had a heart attack on that toilet and died."

"WHOA!"

What I liked best about this story was that it was about a ghost taking a dump. In other words, too ridiculous to be made up.

We were up past midnight, and the strong coffee and Puerto Rican pancakes he made for breakfast the next day took only the barest edge off my hangover. But I left his house smiling. A headache is a small price to pay for the knowledge that even in these contentious times, ghosts are more powerful than conflicting political beliefs.

And everyone knows ghosts aren't even real!

*

I stopped to pay my respects at a statue of Harriet Tubman. She's been one of my heroes ever since I saw "Drunk History" and learned that an illiterate Black woman in the year 1863 led a military raid that freed 750 people in a single night. That's in addition to the 300 slaves she freed on the Underground Railroad. She sang spirituals to communicate coded messages and traveled at night in the winter through swamps. I mean, can you even imagine?

On one trip, a particularly stubborn guy decided the journey was futile and threatened to leave. Harriet knew this would endanger the entire mission, but she wasn't worried. People like this guy were why she carried a pistol. She pointed it at his head and said, "You go on or you die."

And that's why, in 19 trips, Harriet Tubman never lost a person.

An older man joined me at the statue. He had a gray tuft of a beard and wore suspenders and struck up a friendly conversation with me. His name was Willie.

"It was so hard back in slavery times," he said looking up at Harriet Tubman. "Just thinking about what those people went through..."

"The resistance is so inspiring," I said. "This is a part of our history."

"No," he corrected me gently. "This *is* our history."

Harriet Tubman was probably around 10 years old when Oberlin College became the first American university to admit a Black student. Slavery was still legal — and would be for three more decades — but this institution recognized not only these people's humanity, but also their talent. Two years later, Oberlin made history again by admitting a woman. Our right to vote was still 82 years away.

Meanwhile, President Andrew Jackson was busy orchestrating the Trail of Tears. We all know Andrew Jackson, of course, as the man on the $20 bill.

At the International Women's Air & Space Museum in Cleveland, I learned that Amelia Earhart was the first woman to fly solo across the Atlantic. I was shocked. All this time, I thought her big contribution to history was that she disappeared.

And I hadn't even *heard* of Bessie Coleman. She grew up in a family of sharecroppers and walked four miles to a one-room segregated schoolhouse every day. She wanted to learn how to fly, but no American school would educate her because she was Black and Native American. With the help of a couple benefactors and the money she earned as a manicurist and a waitress, she went to France and got her pilot's license in 1921.

She spent her career as a barnstormer, performing daring stunts, and made it her mission to be a positive role model for other people of color.

Maybe the reason that so many gals are too afraid to fly is because they don't know about the paths their ancestors blazed in the sky.

Oberlin College
63 days · 2,468 miles
Hi Friday!

Hello Madam. How are you?

> I'm doing well! I visited Oberlin College. It is located in a small city with many trees and fields. Oberlin is progressive, which means it is known for trying to improve the world. It also has a very good music program!

That's great Madam. Zikomo kwambiri. Hmm.

*

Later on, when the light was deep and gold and the shadows stretched long, I was starting to get that ol end-of-the-day, where-am-I-gonna-sleep anxiety. Turns out Ohio's pretty flat and doesn't have a lot of trees, which adds a whole other level of stealth to stealth camping. It's such a vulnerable feeling, searching for a place to sleep along the road.

I passed a man and woman working in their front yard, and they gave me a friendly wave. I was struck with a pang of longing. Just some nice, normal people finishing up their chores. Probably getting ready to go inside and eat dinner in a cozy dining room. And here I was, all alone, looking for a place to pitch my tent before it got dark.

I should ask them if I can camp in their yard, I thought.

No, don't, I thought.

But they seem nice! They actually acknowledged me.

Don't be a freeloader.

For camping in their yard?

The road ahead crested and sank through empty farmland.

You know what? Worst that happens, they say no, and I'm no worse off than I am right now.

And so I doubled back. They gave me a smile as I stopped at the foot of their driveway.

"Excuse me," I said. "Can I ask you a question? My name is Brooke, and I'm biking across the country. I'm looking for a place to camp for the night. Could I camp in your backyard?"

"Only if you agree to play for our high school basketball team!" laughed the man.

And that's how I met Ken and Nancy.

Without a trace of hesitation, they offered me a spot in their yard… and a shower, a conversation, a giant bag of snacks, and a $200 donation to Represent the Village.

I lay in my tent that night and laughed at myself. Back in Oberlin, I'd perused satellite photos and asked a waitress where the safest place to camp might be. But when I decided to just wing it, a pair of complete strangers gave me $200. More than that, they gave me sanctuary. They extended kindness to someone who was lonely and afraid.

I don't think kindness is inherent. Nor, for that matter, is cruelty. Or maybe they both are, lying dormant in our nature like seeds in the earth. What I *do* think is inherent is our power to choose which of these qualities to cultivate. But what is kindness without someone to receive it? By asking for help, and accepting it with gratitude and grace, we're giving kindness a place to grow.

*

The waitress and the old-timer at the counter were talking about me.

"She's going across the country! Isn't that something?"

"Does she have a gun?" he grumbled.

"I don't know… She didn't mention it."

"Do you have a gun?" the guy demanded across the restaurant.

"No sir!" I said with a smile.

He scowled and turned back to the waitress. "She's crazy," I heard him spit. "She's going to get herself killed."

Here's what I wish I could have told him:

"I don't travel with a weapon, because I feel like that's telling the universe I expect to have to use it. Without a weapon, violence ceases to be an option, and I have to find other ways to protect myself.

"But unarmed doesn't mean defenseless, because force is not the only form of strength. In the tarot, Strength is depicted as a woman smiling calmly and gently holding a lion's mouth open. The Tao describes the strength of softness: 'As a rule, whatever is fluid, soft, and yielding will overcome whatever is rigid and hard.' This is the strength I practice.

"I may not be able to throw a punch, but I can smile and speak calmly. I can listen and speak encouragements and make people feel good about themselves. Don't start no shit, won't be no shit, as the saying goes. I practice my compassion and give others a place to practice theirs, and then I am surrounded in a protective cloak of goodwill, safe as a turtle in her shell."

But come on, nobody talks like that.

Jon and Judah both have the straight posture and wide smiles of youth pastors. Judah has fire in his eyes; Jon has sparkles.

They're brothers. Judah is young, fresh out of college, vocally Christian. Jon is older by 10 years or so. I'll talk to him later, and find out that he used to be like Judah, believing literally in the Bible as the word of god. These days his belief system involves holy galactic overlords. He's one of those people who seems to know something the rest of us don't, something that makes him view life like it's an infinitely precious joke.

He's taking his brother on a cross-country bike trip to show him the world. They started three days ago, and I can sense a friendly sort of friction between them. Brotherly love.

It feels so nice to talk about the journey with other pilgrims, to compare experiences and what we've learned and why we're out here in the first place. I tell them about Ken and Nancy, my meeting at Oberlin, and of course, my students.

"When were you in the Peace Corps?" Jon asks.

"Until 2015."

"Do you know Dmitri?" he asks.

```
                    *

                     *

              *

                  *

         *

            *

                *

                  *

            *


        boom.
```

"I knew him very well," I say softly. Cautiously, I ask, "How is he?"

They look down at the ground, but then Jon smiles and says, "He definitely went through a dark period."

My stomach sinks with guilt. I forgot how very guilty Dmitri made me feel.

"He came and lived with us for a while."

I knew it, I knew his parents kicked him out. He hinted at it but never told me outright, but of course they kicked him out. Remember his room, how dark it was, how the smell was like a solid thing that oozed out of that darkness?

"But now, he's getting his master's degree — where is he, somewhere in Scandinavia, right?"

"Sweden," Judah says.

He's alive, thank god — oh my god — I can breathe again! Have I really been holding my breath for two years?

I'm so relieved. Ever since I last talked to Dmitri, I'd wondered periodically if he was still alive. Two years. That's the length of a Peace Corps contract.

"Wow. *Wow.* That's such a relief. I'm so happy to hear that, you have no idea…" I say. "I just can't believe this… I mean… What are the odds that we'd just happen to run into each other on this bike path, and you'd just happen to know a person I used to be close to?"

Judah looks at me as if to say, "Do I need to connect the dots for you?"

Jon's eyes just sparkle.

*

I was afraid to go to Detroit, so I went to Detroit.

From what I had heard about it (from people who hadn't been there), I was expecting… I don't know, a smoking crater? A war zone?

But when I passed the road sign that welcomed me to Detroit, it was just... empty. There were abandoned buildings and potholes, and above me a cloud of gulls that swooped to land in the parking lot to my right. I have never seen so many gulls in one place. It felt like an omen, but not ominous.

That night, I stayed in the Mexicantown neighborhood with Phil and Stevie. They live on a tree-lined street with old-fashioned houses and kids playing ball in the street. Stevie is a cannonball of a woman, and Phil has a big cartoon nose and a wide smile. They had been itinerant artists, but they fell in love with Detroit and bought a house for less than some people might spend on a car or a year of college education. Now they're artists *and* community organizers.

The next day, Phil and I went for a bike ride. He told me all about Detroit and the adventures he's been on. Back in the '70s, he tossed 30 pounds of stuff into a backpack, hopped on a garage-sale bike, and took off on a tour with an unemployed philosophy professor he'd just met. (I'd watch that movie, wouldn't you?) It felt like a fun father-daughter day. He treated me to good coffee and pastries, gave me sound advice, and when we parted ways, told me if I *ever* needed *anything*, I could call him.

I spent the afternoon at the Heidelberg Project, a spooky outsider art installation that swallows up an entire street. Houses emblazoned with random numbers, big pieces of plywood with YOU painted on them, a cairn of broken bricks in front of Donald Trump in clown makeup and the words WAKE UP!

The brainchild of Tyree Guyton, his wife Karen, and his grandfather Sam Mackey, it was maybe 60% creepy and 30% cool. The remaining 10% was appreciation for the artistic urge in general, and for the fact that Detroit was basically a blank canvas its residents could transform any way they liked.

I spent my second evening with Liam and Liz, a couple of hipsters around my age living in a house that I could have bought with two month's salary as a lunchlady in Antarctica. They were fixing it up together, which I loved. When they were done, every part of that house — from the tub to the banister to the light switch covers — would be a testament to the love they share.

We went to a rooftop Pride party, tossed back some drinks, and danced our asses off. Riding back, a little buzzed, with the warm night air and the city lights streaking past, I thought: Detroit is potential. A (flawed?) place where love can grow.

*

When I first met Suzette, she seemed like your typical successful type. Probably played sports in college and studied something useful. Smart, funny, kind, and beautiful — the kind of person who has it all under control.

She offered me her apartment for the night, but not before taking me out to dinner first. And she shared her story with me.

Three years back, her brother was biking across the country to raise money for affordable housing when he was struck and killed by a distracted driver. It was devastating; he was her hero and best friend. So the next year, she and a group of people who loved him rode their bikes from Deadhorse, Alaska to Key West, Florida. 8,000 miles in eight months. It must have hurt, but she didn't try to escape the pain. She grabbed it by the handlebars instead. And in doing so, she transformed it into hope. I got an immense sense of strength from her, like I was sitting in the palm of a giant.

*

Laura was the first and only solo female touring cyclist I met on my trip, and I was her first too. Lest you think I'm a badass, this girl finished a ride across Australia and decided she wasn't ready to go back home to France yet, so she flew to L.A. and biked to New York City, by way of Michigan.

"This is my first tour," I told her.

"Do you like it?" she asked.

"I love this life."

She nodded and smiled. "This is the freedom life."

*

If you're passing through Indiana Dunes National Park, you'll come upon a neighborhood where a log cabin shares a street with an art deco house the color of strawberry ice cream. Just down the way is a sprawling eyesore in glass and chrome known as the House of Tomorrow. These relics of the 1933-34 Chicago World's Fair were transported by truck and barge across Lake Michigan to this, their permanent home in Beverly Shores, Indiana.

America, you quirky ol' gal, you're not so bad sometimes.

*

A PTA-looking woman walked up on me rolling a joint on a park bench, but I played it cool and we ended up talking about bike touring.

"When you're old like me, you can't do this kind of thing anymore," she told me.

"Not necessarily!" I offered brightly. "Some of the best hikers on the AT were the older guys. They just take it slow and steady, day after day."

She looked at me doubtfully. "You'll see when you're older."

All the more reason, I thought, *to do these things while you're as young as you'll ever be.*

*

The first thing I noticed about the cashier at SciFi Donuts was that she apologized for things that weren't her fault.

"Hey! What's your favorite doughnut here?"

"Oh, um, sorry, I don't really like doughnuts. But a lot of people like the chocolate one? I'm sorry."

As an inveterate apologizer myself, my first thought was, *So that's what I sound like.*

"Um, if you don't mind me asking, is that your bike outside?"

"Sure is."

"Oh, wow. Can I ask how far you're going?"

She carried herself cautiously, as if she were trying not to make too much noise or take up too much space, and she was beautiful in a way she hadn't grown into yet. Like a puppy with big paws, or a soul that's older than the body it inhabits. *Is this… what I was like when I was 17?* I thought.

I told her about my trip and her eyes widened. "Wow. That's so brave. Um, have you ever heard of Isabelle Eberhardt?"

"Can't say I have."

"Oh, um, well, your story reminds me of that. There's a quote from *The Nomad*, which is a collection of her diaries, that goes 'A nomad I will remain for life, in love with distant and uncharted places.'"

There was a lovely pause.

"Sorry, I probably got that wrong."

"What? No, that's amazing!"

"If you don't mind me asking, what do you do when you're not doing this? Like your occupation or what you do for money, I mean?"

"I do seasonal work, most recently in Antarctica. It's nice because I get paid to be in these incredible places, and if I'm smart with my money, I can take time off to go on adventures and do whatever I want."

"Oh, wow. Antarctica, really? Have you read *Terra Incognita*?"

There were no other customers, so she sat with me at a table and told me a bit about herself. She was about to start her senior year of high school.

"What do you want to do when you graduate?"

"Um, it's stupid and weird but... I want to be a social worker?"

"That's not stupid, that's admirable."

"Oh, sorry," she said. "UW Madison has a really good social work program, but, you know, my parents don't want me to go out of state. They want me to stay here where it's safe and they can keep an eye on me."

You know that phrase, "my heart went out"? That's exactly what I felt when she told me that. My heart stretched out of my chest and reached for hers.

I was going to dedicate this book to Jill, since she's always been my biggest inspiration (and toughest competition). But it felt wrong, and I got to thinking: A dedication is the person the book is *for*, and this book isn't for Jill. The gal who went to all-night forest raves with acid-tripping underground DJs in Japan doesn't need me to tell her she can chase her dreams.

So who is it for, I wondered? And I thought back over my trip and all the people I met, and I realized this book is for Emily.

Hey, Emily? When I was your age, I never would have imagined that I'd actually end up being a traveler. I believed all the people who told me "You can't do it." I wish I could get in a time machine and tell 17-year-old me not to listen to those people, and save her a few years of fruitless searching. I'll never get another shot at 17, but at least I can share my truth with you:

Emily, all those people who tell you you can't do it? Who think they know you better than you do? Who think they're justified in telling you how to live your life?

They're fucking wrong.

Go live your dream, Emily. You deserve that, and nothing less.

---

how to live your dream

1. Dream. Dream wildly. Think of a dozen different dreams you'd like to live.

   (Not sure how to dream? Think about what excites or interests you — juggling, skydiving, love, politics — and try the inner child/deathbed test: Ask your inner child if they want to do XYZ. If they get excited, do it. Or picture yourself on your deathbed, saying, "I wish I'd done XYZ." If it rings true, do it.)

2. Now pick one. Any one will do.

3. Research what you need to do to accomplish it. (There is always a way.)

4. Tell everyone you know that you're going to live your dream. That way if you back out, you'll look like a total asshole.

   (Here's where the Dream-Killers are gonna tell you all the reasons why you can't live your dream, all the ways you'll fail, and all the horrible things that will happen to you if you try. **Listen to them and smile.** They don't know it, but their words are the most powerful dream fuel that exists.)

5. Take the first step. Now you're in it.

6. There will be hurdles. Bound over them, every single one of them, just as high as you can, with the biggest smile on your face, and say, "Thank you! What else would you like me to do?"

7. In time, you will find you are living your dream.

This will change your life. If you're living your dream, then it stands to reason that *your life is a dream.* (It's not a metaphor.

Your life is a lucid dream that you are free to shape and explore in any way you like.)

Once you've lived one dream, the others don't seem as far out of reach. So you live another. And another. And sure, not every dream is how you'd envisioned it, and sometimes your plans fall apart, but that's how dreaming works.

Pretty soon, you can't imagine why you'd do anything else. Life is short, after all. But life is also long. How many dreams can you stitch into it? Why not make it as many as you can? Wouldn't it be nice, as you pass from this world to the next, to look back on a patchwork of purpose and passion?

How does that make your inner child feel? Mine is so excited that her fingers are dancing.

Chicago, Ill.
71 days · 3,018 miles

Olive Oil and I hiked together on the Appalachian Trail for the first 500 miles. She seemed like an unlikely thru-hiker: a bubbly, flawlessly beautiful vegetarian and recent Cornell grad. We got absorbed into different Trail families, and hers slowed down while mine pulled ahead. When she caught up (and then passed me) in Massachusetts, she had sent home her sleeping pad to save weight. After hiking 20+ miles a day, this girl would sleep in a bivvy bag with only the cold, hard ground as a mattress. My first impression had been completely wrong: This was one of the toughest human beings I'd ever met.

But that transformation is what makes it so jarring to meet back up with your Trail friends. On a thru-hike, the longer you get to know a person, the scragglier, skinnier, stronger, dirtier, and more feral they get. Even on town days, after a shower and a meal or two, they still have that wild look in their eyes. Seeing them again in the real world after a few years, it's like you've hit rewind. They've lost that hardness; they're clean, gainfully employed, productive members of society. They live in houses now — or in Olive Oil's case, in a high-rise in downtown Chicago with a door code and cucumber water in the lobby.

As I nervously knocked on her apartment door, I had to wonder: Without the shared experience of the Trail, would Olive Oil and I have anything to talk about?

"SLIM RIMS!!!!"

"OLIVE OIL!!!!"

"I'm so glad you're here! Come in! There are towels in the bathroom, and dinner's almost ready, and I'm so happy to see you! You look great! This is so exciting, I can't wait to hear all about your trip!"

Oh, that's right. Olive Oil is the most effusive, authentic, effortlessly kind person on the planet.

*

The next day started off with such promise. I pedaled up to Evanston along a lakeside bike path, reveling in the unencumbered freedom of biking without all 60 pounds of gear sagging in my panniers. Like taking off a heavy backpack and standing up straight.

I ate macaroons and drank coffee at an adorable Parisian café, and told the baker they were a beautiful human.

"Aww, that really touched my life!" they said.

The counselor at Northwestern seemed impressed by my journey and excited to hear from Friday. He told me grit matters and gave me the best college admissions essay advice I've ever heard: No poems. To celebrate another successful meeting, I got some deep-dish and drew some comics I was proud of. Jon with the sparkling eyes had commented on one of my Instagram posts that we were going to be in Chicago at the same time. In an impulsive moment of bravery, I asked if he'd like to get tea and hang out later.

"I'd love that!" he responded immediately.

This day kept getting better. All I had left was my meeting at the University of Chicago. I had high hopes: It seems like the kind of place that nurtures good ideas, even and especially the unorthodox ones. I mean, just look at these admissions essay questions:

What's so odd about odd numbers?

— *Inspired by Mario Rosasco, AB '09*

Fans of the movie *Sharknado* say that they enjoy it because "it's so bad, it's good." Certain automobile owners prefer classic cars because they "have more character." And recently, vinyl record sales have skyrocketed because it is perceived that they have a warmer, fuller sound. Discuss something that you love not in spite of but rather due to its quirks or imperfections.

— *Inspired by Alex Serbanescu, Class of 2021*

Find x.

— *Inspired by Benjamin Nuzzo, an admitted student from Eton College, UK*

Earth. Fire. Wind. Water. Heart! Captain Planet supposes that the world is made up of these five elements. We're familiar with the previously noted set and with actual elements like hydrogen, oxygen, and carbon, but select and explain another small group of things (say, under five) that you believe compose our world.[21]

— *Inspired by Dani Plung, class of 2017*

But when I got to the admissions office — after 40 miles of biking — I was told the counselor on duty was busy for the rest of the day.

"Would you like to leave a message?"

"But... um... I biked here from Raleigh?"

---

[21] You better believe I spent a lot of time turning this over in my head. The best I could come up with was love, fear, luck, and fate.

I felt preposterous.

The receptionist took pity on me and found a counselor for me to talk to. He didn't work with international students; he just wasn't busy and could afford to waste 20 minutes. He stared at me politely while I rushed through the broad strokes of my presentation. I was living in the worst-case scenario I had been so afraid of at the beginning of my trip.

You know that feeling when it's time to go to the gym, but you don't *wanna* go to the gym, you wanna stay on the couch and eat cookies? And then you force yourself to put on your shoes and go to the fucking gym... and it sucks just as much as you thought it would? So you pointlessly go through the motions until your workout is over and then go back to eating cookies on the couch? That was what this meeting was.

But you know what? Those are the most important workouts of all. They're the ones where you could have given up but didn't.

Over tea that night, Jon and I talked about spirituality, family, love, and what makes life meaningful. He quoted Walt Whitman and said god was an alien. I think in another life, we could have been friends. But he was biking south the next day, and I was heading west. He had his brother and his direction; I had myself and mine.

On the Appalachian Trail, you're part of a community. Everyone you meet has the same destination (even though every journey is different, and isn't *that* a beautiful concept). But there was no community of cyclists connecting the dots of Ivy League universities that summer. There was just me.

Biking back to Olive Oil's place through the city lights and city darkness, I thought about how nice it would be to share this trip with someone. I thought about Maple, how she's perpetually steering away from the people we care about, even as Fiddlehead is moaning, *Noooo, why are we doing this again?*

Because then we're safe, Maple insists.

"We meet at meals three times a day, and give each other a new taste of that old musty cheese that we are," wrote Thoreau. Better to make myself scarce, to protect those people I care about from that musty cheese that I am, to protect myself from rejection. Let my every interaction be new and disposable. If they go well, there's a person in the world who thinks I'm an eidolon. And if not, I need never see them again. On the outside of a turtle's shell, intricate swirls. On the inside, the world.

*

I sat slumped on a boulder on the side of a bike path, crying openly and eating not one but two cinnamon-chip scones.

As you can imagine, absolutely no one acknowledged me. People in the city are good at pretending they don't see a giant woman with tears rolling out from her sunglasses eating not one but two cinnamon-chip scones. Maybe they assumed that I had this situation under control.

Or maybe I was a ghost!

I had absolutely nothing under control. My life was a swirling vortex. I had spent the last hour trying to leave the city, but I kept getting lost and ending up in the same place a quarter-mile from Olive Oil's house. It felt like a maddening dream.

I felt *so lonely*.

I had to say goodbye to a friend, and I wasn't going to see another one until Miles City, Montana. I met a person who felt connected to the same reality as me, and then I had to say goodbye to him too. I checked my email and Dmitri from the Peace Corps had sent me a message. Jon and Judah must have told him they'd met me. I couldn't bear to open the email because the sight of his name made me feel like I'd chugged a pitcher of ice water. The worst part was how *familiar* it felt. This was how I felt when we were still talking, I realized with shock. How had I managed to convince myself that this was *okay*?

I slumped and sighed and let the tears crawl down my cheeks. Gazed over at Lucky, my sole companion. Felt like an animal at the zoo. My every action was public, and no one knew my name.

But.

I eventually found my way out of the city. The skyscrapers shrunk to suburbs that sank into unburnished land. I rode past tall grass and chain-link fences, through soft drifts of cottonwood fluff, to a town called Zion. The bike path dwindled to dirt and finally led me to a lonely little scrap of beach with smooth stones the color of olive oil and Himalayan sea salt, beneath a sunset like weak herbal tea.

I locked my bike, set up my tent, and crawled inside. Sighed. *I'm sad. I recognize and honor that.* And I told myself the ups and downs are two sides of the same coin. Trust the setbacks, ride them out. Without loneliness, friendship wouldn't mean a thing.

Is it hard to ride your bike across the country?

On nights like this one it is.

*

In my dream, there was a roar like a gas station hand dryer and birds were flapping against my face. My body came to life before my brain caught up, and I woke myself up swiping the air. I blinked hard and saw yellow nylon pummeling my face.

My tent was moving — shuddering and wriggling like a cat trying to escape a hug. I grabbed hold of the wall and held it still enough to peer through the bug netting. The pieces clicked into place: A massive cloudbank was charging over the lake, and the trees were bowed over in the roaring wind.

I shot out of my tent like it was on fire and crashed through the bushes toward... I have no idea where. I wasn't even

170

wearing a bra. And then, finally, Maple woke up enough to take the steering wheel.

What are you doing, she said flatly. *Girl, you have a bicycle, remember?*

Oh.

So I put on my shoes, braced my tent with driftwood and rocks, yelled over the shrieking wind, "GOOD LUCK, TENT!" and then chased my headlight toward a stand of trees. Maybe I could hunker in there, wait out the worst of it, and then go back for my tent once it was over.

And then I saw a beacon of hope: An outhouse!

I careened over and tried the door — it was open! — and turned on the light. The floor was concrete but clean. No spiders, no bugs, and the toilet even had a lid. As far as outhouses go, this was a palace. I gave a cheer of victory, leaned Lucky against the wall, put down the lid and had a seat.

After a moment, I thought, *Sleeping pad'd be pretty nice right about now.*

And so I rode like a madwoman back into the wild, windy night; rolled tent, pad, and sleeping bag together into a big sloppy burrito that I stuffed into a pannier; and then tore back just as fast as I could, cackling and breathless with the exhilaration of it all.

As soon as I set up my sleeping arrangement, the storm hit. You know how you count the seconds between the thunder and the lightning, and that tells you how far away the lightning is? There was no counting on that night. It was lightningthundering, just like that, linked like zipper teeth. And me cheering from my bed on the outhouse floor.

Before this trip, I probably couldn't imagine a scenario in which I'd be grateful — profoundly so — to sleep in an outhouse. But that night, I was giddy. There's a special kind of relief that comes from knowing you've hit bottom. I mean, this was undoubtedly the worst place I was going to sleep all trip. And if I was this happy to be in the worst place... I could handle anything that might come my way.

*

The next morning I biked along Lake Michigan sloshing like an overfull bowl and gleaming like chipped nail polish. The world around me was revitalized, like it had just woken up from a good sleep. Like all its histrionics last night hadn't even happened. I tried to scowl but broke into a giant grin. *I can't stay mad at you*, I thought.

Passing a smiling woman out for a walk with her dog, I called out, "Good morning! Are we in Wisconsin?"

"Yes we are!"

"Woo-hoo!"

"Yup! We're in Pleasant Prairie, Wisconsin."

This is why I love the adventuring life. Something as simple as finding out you're in Wisconsin is enough to make you cheer.

---

snapshots: wisconsin

I napped on a raft in the middle of a sparkling lake, ate s'mores for dinner, and added "a partially constructed, one-room lake house with no electricity" to my list of places I've slept.

*

Here's what you tell yourself when you have _____ miles to go:

86-110: All right! Big day! Let's *do* this!

41-85: Hey, it's an average day! You've done this a million times!

27-40: Pssh, this is the kind of mileage you were doing when you first got started. Look how far you've come!

26: Just a marathon to go! Imagine if you had to *run* this? Now *that* would be hard. You *got* this!

13-25: Almost there!

5-12: Hey, we made it! We're basically there! That wasn't bad at all!

Yep, that's all there is to bike touring: good ol positive thinking and self-encouragement... that is, until you get to mile 4. At mile 4, some horrible trick of quantum physics kicks in, every mile turns into 10 miles, and you're left with only one thought, which is:

0-4: FFFFFFFFFFFFFFFFFFFFFFFFFFFFFFU-

*

I got caught in a crushing rainstorm on a residential street, so I pulled over to a random house and knocked on the door.

"Hi! I'm riding my bike across the country. Can I wait out this rain on your porch?"

"What? Of course not, you're coming inside!"

And I sipped coffee with Dawn and Herb until the rain stopped.

Mt. Horeb, Wisc.
77 days · 3,352 miles

Mt. Horeb's claim to fame is the collection of carved wooden trolls that line the streets. They're worth checking out, if you're ever in that area. Some of them are cool and quirky, and some of them are pure nightmare fuel. But what charmed me most about Mt. Horeb was a modest little playground called Grandma Foster Park. According to a brass plaque on a mossy rock:

This park is dedicated
to the memory of
MRS. JOHN FOSTER
who loved little children
and animals.

That's just about the nicest legacy I can think of.

diner break: schubert's (mt. horeb, wis.)

So your hot fruit soup from Sjolind's Chocolate House didn't quite hit the spot? Come on down the street to Schubert's!

This building has been a diner for 108 years. Just imagine! 108 years of fresh coffee and frying bacon. 108 years of people taking off jackets and shaking off sleep to belly up to the counter or slide into a booth. 108 years of diner conversation, boisterous old guys, sassy old dames, parents scolding their kids, travelers rolling through town, a gal in the corner booth hunched over a notebook, smiling and quietly taking it all in.

When's the last time you heard a new sound?

I was biking past a field when suddenly there was this musical knocking noise I'd never heard before. I whirled around; in the tall grass to my right was a trio of giant birds the color of pencil shavings or coffee with too much skim milk.

Seeing a crane up close is like... is that a dinosaur? They're as tall as middle schoolers and their legs bend backward and they have melted red masquerade masks over their eyes. And then hearing them it's like... is that an *alien* dinosaur? Their voices sound like toppling toy blocks or lazy waves knocking around under a wooden raft. One of them spread its wings and bobbed at me.

I was instantly fascinated, and fell down a deep Wikipedia rabbit hole that night. Did you know demoiselle cranes — which are only 3 feet tall and weigh 7 pounds — migrate over the Himalayas at heights of up to 26,000 feet? Or that blue cranes are so revered by the Zulu of southern Africa that only royalty are allowed to wear blue crane feathers? How about that the Brolga crane has a special gland that essentially allows it to cry out excess salt from the saltwater it drinks?

A few days later when I found a pamphlet for a place called the International Crane Foundation, there wasn't even a question of whether I was going to bike 40 miles out of my way to check it out. Wikipedia is great and all, but nothing beats the real thing.

Not only did I get to see every crane species in the world, I also made friends with the tour guide, Chris. At first he offered to let me spend the night at his apartment, but it was 20 miles back the way I'd come. So he called up a friend who owns an organic farm farther on down the road. I ended my day eating rhubarb cobbler with Carissa, a human so free she tells time by the sun and the season, not a clock or a calendar.

As I fell asleep on Carissa's couch with her half-blind orange cat purring softly on my chest, I got to thinking: Those cranes could have just been part of the landscape, a passing curiosity and nothing more. But instead, I let myself be carried away by my interest, and it led me to a place to sleep. Life rewards those who trust themselves.

*

It's overcast, the light pallid gray, and I am alone except for the low hum of far-off traffic. Up ahead and drawing closer is a tunnel cut into a hillside, framed by two great wooden doors thrown open as if to say, "Welcome, traveler." I peer inside; there is the glassy sound of dripping water and the smell of wet stone.

Ooh, spooky! my brain thinks. *Let's go!*

wutever you say, boss, thinks my body. She takes a step in and then freezes. It's such a sharp disconnect between intention and instinct that I almost laugh.

don't wanna do this, Body mumbles.

What are you talking about? Brain snaps.

... scared.

Body is quietly shocked that idiot Brain doesn't recognize such an obvious threat. Brain is exasperated that idiot Body has frozen at something so obviously benign. But Body isn't budging, so Brain rolls her eyes and starts churning out solutions.

I could call Rob... nope, no cell service in a tunnel. If I turn around, that's an extra... god, like 20 miles, on busy roads. Body, are you sure we can't do this?

Body is silent. My stomach feels heavy.

And then Brain, throwing up her hands, thinks the thing a strong, independent woman is never, ever supposed to think (but that is beginning to feel like a familiar refrain on this trip): *Ugh, I wish there was a guy here to walk with me.*

I could picture it exactly. My ex and I roll up to the tunnel, and I hesitate at the entrance. He notices I'm afraid, and teases me in his gentle way, and holds my hand as we walk through. Midway through the tunnel, I realize I've made a big deal out of nothing, but it's too late. He helped me overcome my fear. We emerge together, our bond stronger than it was before we entered. For the rest of our trip — our lives? — whenever we encounter a tunnel, he teases me in that gentle way. And that is how I am defined: As the girl who's afraid of tunnels, but thank god my boyfriend is there to help me through.

Well, that ain't an option right now.

Remember the pink bandana, Brain says. *We have been through some shit together before, and we always make it out okay. So listen to me: This is a tunnel that little kids ride through on their bikes. There's nothing to be afraid of, I promise you. Together we are brave enough to do this.*

Body is silent, but the weight in my stomach is lifting. My brow furrows, my jaw sets, my shoulders square. I am Brave Brooke, and this tunnel isn't going to beat me.

I step inside. In the cool darkness, my headlight contracts to a dusty half-moon. I focus on it like it's a shield, and I call upon my secret weapon. The most powerful tool that exists for defusing fear. I'm speaking, of course, of The Flaming Lips.

I sing, just as loud as I can, "Her name is Yoshimi / she's a black belt in karate..."

It's really hard to be scared when you're singing. That's just a fact of life. And if it's a silly song about a karate superhero? All the better. I sing "Yoshimi Battles the Pink Robots," "Do You Realize?," "Waiting for Superman," and "What is the Light?"

"What / is / the light? / That /you / have / shining / all a-/ round you?"

And then I look up and laugh, because there it is: the light at the end of the tunnel, expanded to a dusty thumbprint. I'm almost there. I feel the panicky urge to sprint the rest of the way, but I dismiss it with a deep breath. The hard part is over.

Body is elated. **we did it!!!!!!!!!!!!!!!!!**

Brain smiles wearily, but also overcome. *Yeah gal, we did it.*

This could have been an entry in the book of a relationship. It could have strengthened a bond between me and another human. But it wasn't. Instead, the bond I strengthened was with myself. And that was so much more powerful than me and some dude. I emerged from that tunnel awash in self-love, in the knowledge that I am Brave Brooke, and I can take care of myself.

Alma, Wisc.
81 days · 3,504 miles

I set out into among the silver veils of morning fog with a singular purpose: find coffee.

It had been a long night. And why? Was it the traffic noise? No, that's a given, like the gentle snoring of a lover. Murmuring cars, whining motorcycles, grumbling semis — they might seem like strange bedfellows, but for me, they were a reassurance that I wasn't *all* alone. Same goes for the deer snorting outside my tent. Now that I knew they weren't serial killers, they were just my rude neighbors.

No, if I had to put my finger on it, I'd have to say the reason I was so tired was that I had unwittingly set up camp one thin mile from the Mississippi Thunder Speedway. Racecar-induced insomnia: now there's a first.

Coffee was in order. Mapsy had suggested a gas station on the outskirts of Alma, so I pointed my handlebars in that direction and let my body slog along while my brain tried to sneak a nap behind my open eyes.

Main Street was a garrison of sturdy little buildings with window moldings like unkempt eyebrows and awnings as ruffled as a lampshade in your grandma's house. I spied a white building with giant pretzel and a French flag hanging over the door.

Ooh, it's a bakery, I thought. *I wonder if they're —*

As if on cue, a lanky man in a beret and a white apron stepped outside and hung a wooden sign that said "Open."

Well that answers that, I thought.

The low rhythmic clunking of a tubby industrial mixer, the warm, comforting aroma of baking bread, and a woman who smiled warm as a teapot and told me they weren't quite open yet, but that the coffee was ready and I was welcome to have a seat. The man in the beret was in the back, attending to his various creations.

Over my coffee, I worked on my route plan.

6/26: Montevideo, MN

6/27: Webster, SD

6/28: ???

6/29: Mobridge, SD

I tapped my pen on the paper. There was no way to get around camping on the 28th, and I felt apprehensive. On the east coast, I had some idea of what to expect in terms of animals, landscapes, and people... But South Dakota was a big question mark. I was pretty sure it was open plains, and I was stuck on how to stealth camp without trees. Was I better off sticking to rural areas or maybe small towns where I could camp at a fire department or something?

Hungry for a distraction, I got to chatting with the baker and his wife. Their names were Pete and Marolyn, and they had recently moved to Alma.

"Where from?"

"South Dakota."

"Oh! Well hey, what can you tell me about it? I've never been there before, and I'm gonna need to camp there on my way through."

"We have a house in Aberdeen that you're welcome to use," Marolyn said off-handedly. "Our son lives there, and they're always hosting people."

"That's so nice of you!" I said. "But South Dakota's a big state, and I have kind of a tight schedule..."

Marolyn just smiled mischievously, like she knew something I didn't. "What route are you taking?"

"Uh..." I glanced down at the map. "Route 12."

And then I saw it: Aberdeen. Almost exactly halfway between Webster and Mobridge.

"Whoa!" I said. "You're not gonna believe this. Aberdeen is *exactly* where I would have camped!"

"Really?" Pete asked. He seemed as blown away as I was; Marolyn just stood there with that same smile on her face.

"I can't believe this. What are the odds!"

"Want to hear the really strange part?" Pete asked. "We don't usually open for another hour and a half. I just had the urge to open early today."

"WHAT."

Marolyn looked at me and winked. "God's got your back, girl," she said.

*

I rolled into Minnesota and up and down the steep pitches of a road tracing the Mississippi River, singing my heart out to The Mountain Goats' *Tallahassee*. It's a wrenching (but also at times gleeful) album about a doomed relationship between two shattered humans dragging each other deep down beneath the waves of Hood River Gin.

I bet it's gotten a lot of people through a lot of breakups.

Funny enough, the first time I encountered this album, I too was in a doomed relationship. And he did in fact live in Tallahassee! If only I had known that this album had traveled through the collective unconscious to warn me[22], I could have saved myself a few years of anguish. Instead, I was like, "This music is boring!" When we did actually break up, I got through it with Kanye West, realizing he was never good enough for me, and abandoning my boring life to go on adventures.

Can that be a new fairy tale? Girl gets dumped by guy, realizes he was a chain around her neck almost the whole time, becomes a badass, and lives happily ever after?

Even though *Tallahassee* is probably most deeply felt as a breakup album, it weirdly also worked on that day in Minnesota. There was something deeply validating about being a single gal on a solo adventure, secure in her self-reliance, singing merrily along to the soundtrack of the ghost of the last time she ever let a man hold her back.

*

So anyway, let's talk about public urination.

Don't get me wrong, this wasn't a choice. Necessity is the mother of public urination, as the saying goes, and by god Minnesota made it necessary. Bigger miles between smaller

---

[22] John Darnielle has this preternatural ability to write songs that so perfectly capture certain moments in my life, I wonder if he's spying on me. Or maybe, just maybe, my experiences aren't all that unique! And this, I think, is the finest message that art can convey: You are not alone.

towns (I once passed a road sign reading "Cedar Mills, Pop. 45") and not even so much as a bush to duck behind. What's a lady to do?

I devised an elegant solution. I'd wait for a break in traffic, then squat next to my bike, spread my dress around me, and "carefully inspect my bike chain." Perhaps an astute driver may have noticed that my bike had sprung an alarming leak, but if they did, well... fuck em. This is what it means to be wild.

*

Peggy and Sam are giddily in love, having both abandoned the sinking ships of their previous marriages. Peggy is eternally youthful, a born storyteller, charming me with mile-a-minute anecdotes while Sam quietly roasts asparagus and grills chicken.

After dinner we sit on tall stools around their kitchen counter, and Sam tells stories about his college days in Durham.

"There was this farmhouse where, oh, 20 or 30 people would show up and play music. One night, there was this quiet guy in the corner, playing guitar and singing. He was good, but no one knew who he was or who invited him."

"Huh."

"So the next night, we go to see this concert, who was it... Doesn't matter, but the opener's this guy no one's ever heard of, James Taylor. It was that quiet guy in the corner!"

"You're kidding!"

"Our jaws just dropped," he chuckles, shaking his head. "Another time, Janis Joplin was in town, but after her show, a snowstorm cancelled all the flights out. I don't know how she heard about our farmhouse, but sure enough, she showed up."

"WHAT! What was Janis Joplin like?"

Definitively, he says, "She had a bottle of whiskey in the pocket of her skirt and she was full of herself."

*

The next morning, I found myself at Carleton College, a small, well-respected liberal arts institution and the last stop on my trip. Brian was kind enough to squeeze me in for a half-hour meeting first thing in the morning. We hit it off immediately; it felt like encountering a fellow English-speaker in a foreign country. Friday's lived experience in the village as an educational resource? Brian got it. The inherent unfairness of a college teaching American kids about global poverty but not educating the poor? Brian was on board. The importance of true diversity on campus, not just admitting a bunch of privileged kids from foreign countries and calling it the same thing? Brian couldn't agree more.

We kept chatting even as we both rose to leave. He had to lead a tour group, he explained apologetically; otherwise he'd love to keep talking.

"No worries! I think we're on the same page, and I can't wait for you to read Friday's application!"

I bounced down the Admissions building stairs and beamed up at the sky. Way back in North Carolina, when I was trying to coax this whole endeavor into reality, I'd been certain no one would take me seriously. And now I was done! Sure, there had been experiences like Columbia and UChicago, but more often than not, I felt like I'd genuinely connected with people, and shared a worthwhile message.

Now that the first part of my journey was over, I could focus on taking care of myself as I headed out into the vast and mythic west.

7

what is freedom?

Montevideo, Minn.

84 days • 3,765 miles

Okay. I've biked 97.4 miles and I have 9.3 to go. That's 93/10ths. If I bike at 10 mph, that's probably... 55 minutes left. If I do 60 rpms, that's... 3,300 more pedals. But I probably only have 92/10ths by now... so how many pedals is that?

It felt like I was sitting on two knives. The pain was well past the point of ignoring or even rationalizing — it could only be endured. Worse than that, the only way to escape the pain was by doing the painful thing for another... call it 53 minutes now, how many pedals is that?

I saw a group of bikers heading my way, and my stomach sank.

"Hey! Are you Brooke?"

It was my Warm Showers host — a kind and generous soul who had agreed to feed and shelter me for the night —and he wanted to take me on the scenic route back to his house.

I tried not to sound too desperate when I asked, "How much farther is it?"

Even though he took pity on me and gave me the abridged version, by the time I dismounted Lucky and hobbled to the house, I had done 106.7 miles. I cannot recall a single detail about the scenic route.

We humans are made of strong stuff.

"I can't believe you had a tailwind the whole darn day!" he told me over dinner.

"I think the weather gods like me!"

I was only half joking. On all my adventures, I've never gotten truly frozen or truly soaked or truly overheated. And now here I was, in the land of the vicious headwind, and I had a tailwind the whole darn day.

This is the truth about me: I believe in the weather gods, and I believe they have blessed me. I think this amuses them, the way you or I might be amused by the antics of a squirrel, and so they tolerate me, but also occasionally send me a violent thunderstorm at midnight to keep me in my place.

And I just laugh and yell thank you up at the clouds.

*

I left Montevideo so early that the streetlights on Main Street were still flashing yellow. Women in dizzyingly patterned tights and sports bras did burpees and mountain climbers in a plaza in the center of town. Watching over them was a bronze statue of a man in knee-high boots and a long coat. His face was resolute, but his hips were cocked slightly, and he held his hat off to the side as if to say, "Proceed."

JOSE ARTIGAS, the plaque read. FATHER OF THE INDEPENDENCE OF URUGUAY.

I love you, America. I love you because you have a statue of Jose Artigas in the middle of a small city in Minnesota.

One of the women spotted me and called out, "How far are you going?"

"Seattle!"

And then this group of women — strong, hard-working women who dragged themselves out of bed at the crack of dawn to do burpees with Jose Artigas — stopped their workouts to cheer and shout encouragement. I was so humbled, grateful, and overcome, all I could do was laugh.

I love you, humanity. I love you because you have a special song you sing for someone who's chasing a dream.

And then I crossed an invisible line into South Dakota. To my left, four mule deer bounded like UFOs over the fringe of the long, silken grass. There is muted magic in the land there, in the way the shadows puddle between the hills and the way the grass ripples in the wind.

The wind.

The ever-present, 10 mph headwind that pushed back against me like it was trying to keep me away.

The weather gods had forsaken me at last, and that wind and I would become intimately acquainted over the next few days.

I took three long breaks that day. The first one was under a railroad bridge, just before Highway 6 hits U.S. 12. A flock of barn swallows — iridescent arrowheads with forked tails — boomeranged back and forth, their indignant cheeping bouncing off the walls. I crouched on the ground and waited to see if they'd eventually forget I was there. No dice. Barn swallows are a discerning lot.

"Thank you for letting me rest in your house," I said softly.

The second one was in a massive, meatlocker-cold truck stop firmly planted at the top of a mountain. A fortification of what we call civilization, swarming with sunburned sightseers, a cacophony of conversation and canned music and morgue-white light and lunatic advertisements shrieking up from every surface.

I took my break and drank a shake that I bought from a machine with a flashing screen. Me and the sightseers were all the same: a flock of swallows seeking shade.

I coasted to the bottom of the hill and took my third break next to the glacial lakes outside Waubay. Mirror-flat and mirror-still, stretching nearly to the horizon, perfect portraits of the sky framed by stones and bare trees and the gentlest nascent undulation of far-off hills. Not a swallow or a sightseer in the whole sacred place.

It was so gorgeous I laughed out loud.

*

For the first time in 1,600 miles, I was having an absurd conversation with friends. The last time this happened was with the Cornell Ph.D.s playing America's favorite game, "What Food Would Be Most Awkward to Bring to a Colloquium?". Here in Aberdeen, among the punks and anarchists, it was about which of them I was going to axe-murder first.

"Why am I an axe-murderer? Is it self-defense?"

"No, you're a drifter. All drifters are axe-murderers."

"Oh, duh... Well, what would be a better strategy: Pick off the weaklings first, or start with your leader?"

Up until this point, it had been a totally normal day... by bike tour standards... which means I fought my way across a wholly unfamiliar landscape against the air turned savage with wind, utterly alone.

"We have a leader? Who's our leader?"

"You tell me..."

"Aha! That's an old axe-murderer trick, don't tell her!"

I stopped at a gas station for a snack, but when I went to pay I realized I'd forgotten my wallet in my sweatshirt pocket at a restaurant 10 miles back. The cashier offered to drive me there. What took an hour on a bike took 15 minutes in a car. It felt like teleportation. It was humbling, maybe even disconcerting, to think that my epic journey could have equated to a leisurely 10-day road trip.

And everything I'd seen, all the people I'd met, all the sweat and suffering and raw joy, would have been a blur through the car window.

(My wallet and sweatshirt were both okay, by the way.)

"If she kills our leader, we'll be so panicked that we'll start killing each other."

"Do your job for you!"

"I'm not gonna lie, that would save me a lot of chopping."

"Yeah, being an axe murderer must be hell on your shoulders."

On a bike tour, the extraordinary becomes a part of the fabric of your daily life. You don't take it for granted, and you *never* expect it. All you can do is accept it as gracefully as you can, the suffering and the kindness both, and say thank you, even and especially when there's no one around to hear it.

But when the extraordinary becomes everyday, the everyday becomes sacred. Buzzed and riding my bike around a small city with a punk-rock kid whose parents took a shine to me when I visited their bakery back in Wisconsin. Ordering a beer in a dive bar and chatting with a girl about her job. Hanging out with a group of people I might have been friends with in another life, drinking Miller High Life and trying to make each other laugh.

"Does your axe have a name?"

"Is it Axe L. Rose?"

Tonight, I didn't have to play the role of the saintly Returned Peace Corps Volunteer on a mission to save the world. Tonight, I just got to be normal.

"You're all wrong, his name is Reginald, and I sent him home to save weight. Hey, so uh, on a totally unrelated topic, anybody got an axe I can borrow?"

Well... relatively normal at least.

---

snapshots: 384th avenue and westward

5 a.m. darkness on a dirt road outside town, and the memory of Aberdeen retreating east.

*

Welcome

to

Bowdle

State's Tallest Water tower

read the first sign. To hammer home the point, there was another sign below it:

T O W E R D A Y S

Last Weekend in June

And below that one:

Pheasant Phest

Fourth Saturday in October

Bowdle, South Dakota is also home to a gas station where you can drink weak coffee, watch the wind rip through the grass, and cry.

Is it hard to ride your bike across the country?

*

I played a game I called "Look at That Tower in the Distance and Don't Take Your Eyes Off It Until You Pass It." It took forever to win and when I did, my prize was a yet more distant tower.

I think there's a reason none of these games catch on.

*

188

What was I doing out here? Just… riding a bike? It felt hollow, selfish. My work for Represent the Village was done. No more inspiring conversations with admissions counselors or updates for Friday. I was beginning to feel lost with just the road ahead to guide me. I had only one destination left: the Seattle airport for my flight to Malawi. The rest of my tour was something to be gotten through. All of this America transformed into a long layover.

What does it mean to chase your dreams?

Playing tag, only with your entire life.

I'm sorry, did I give you the impression that my 5,000-mile bike ride was easy?

*

At day's welcome end, I rode a long downhill under clouds furrowed as a worried brow. The Missouri ran in Van Gogh brushstrokes, cobalt and gray. Squatting on its soft, green banks is Mobridge, a town with the feel of an abandoned lot.

A blanket of clouds in shades of Bic and chicory flower pulled back at the horizon, revealing a soft stripe of peach, the first rays of the rising sun. Beneath it, an aquamarine lake, reeds piercing its surface in acupuncture array. The lone mark of humanity was a green road sign that said

WELCOME TO
THE STANDING ROCK SIOUX
RESERVATION

As the world slowly woke up around me, the clouds blanched to the color of marble, sprayed across the sky like champagne, in a pattern that's never existed and will never exist again. Swallows careened dizzily over a wrinkled lake. The sunlight kissed the hills around me and made them blush auburn and brown. I slid up and down the hills like a stupid toy. The landscape was as gently creased as a soft brioche bun.

I had followed the Standing Rock/Dakota Access Pipeline story closely when it came out. I thought it was yet more colonialism, and utter hypocrisy on the part of the government given its stance on immigration. If the argument is that we have to keep Latinx immigrants out to protect American culture, then how can you support the pollution of Native American land?

That old excuse: "It creates jobs."

The Sioux aren't the enemy here. We're all held hostage by powerful corporations that pay off the government, use force to oppress peaceful protestors, build their damn pipeline, insist it's safe, and when it leaks, count on the fact that by then, public attention will be elsewhere.

*

Six miles outside McIntosh, I was fighting my way uphill. The only sounds were my labored breathing, the howl of the headwind, and a maddening squeak from Lucky's bottom bracket. I'd just had her tuned up in Aberdeen, so I assumed it was nothing, just what happens when you've biked 4,000 miles... until I felt it. A wobble.

I got to the top of the hill and knelt next to Lucky, grabbed the pedal, and gave it a nudge. It wiggled like a tooth that's starting to come loose. It felt like the ball bearing cage might have disintegrated. It was an easy enough fix, as long as I had the right tools... which I didn't. So I took it slow until I got to McIntosh, population 90. There was only one business in town, a gas station with an attached garage. The mechanic wasn't working that day, but the owner let me in. They didn't have the tool I needed

It was 40 miles to Lemmon, a little town on the border of North Dakota. With 2,000 people, the odds were better that there'd be a bike shop there. Lucky could probably make it, but I didn't want to risk damaging her frame. So I hitchhiked.

how to hitchhike

Rule #1: Find a good spot to stand. Cars should be able to see you from a ways away, and there should be enough room for them to pull over. If you can, walk in the direction you're going. It appeals to the people who might otherwise think you're a lazy freeloader.

Rule #2: Radiate good vibes. When you hear a car coming, spin around and smile and walk backward with your thumb out. "Well hey there! Doin' good today? I'm just a gal on an adventure who's hit a minor snag. Can I get a lift?" (Note: It helps to be female. Most people don't view you as a threat, and some people even feel instinctively protective of you.)

Rule #3: Be grateful. If they keep driving, give em a shrug, a smile, and a wave. "Hey, thanks anyway!" Not only is this polite and charming, maybe 1 out of every 20 times, it changes the person's mind. If they stop, don't walk to their car — run, and run joyfully.

Rule #4: Know when to say no.

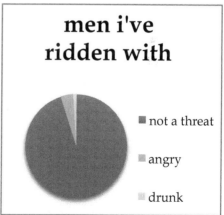

You have 10-15 seconds to decide whether to trust the person who just pulled over. Body language and tone of voice tell you a lot. Most people are totally normal*. Even if someone seems a little sketchy, you can still take a ride from them, but be on your guard.

If you get a bad feeling, say, "I'm sorry, but I don't ride with men**. Thanks for understanding." If he's a good man, he will respect that. If he doesn't, you're still outside his car and you can get away.

Otherwise, hop on in. You're about to have an adventure!

*See Fig. 7.1.
**See Fig. 7.1.

Lemmon, S.D.
88 days · 4,101 miles

On a bike tour, you can pedal through a surreal landscape in the morning, battle mechanical issues in the blazing midday sun, get a lift from a nice married couple in the afternoon, and that evening find yourself on a double-date.

Bruce and I, both over 6 feet tall, were crammed in the backseat of a hatchback making a fumbling attempt at conversation. It was like trying to thumb-wrestle with socks on our hands.

"So, uh, Bruce, are you from around here?"

"No! No, uh, not from here."

"Oh, cool cool..."

Up front were Briana and her date. We'll call him Chad, 'cause he had a Chaddish personality: a snarky, conversational one-upper, the kind of guy you hate to admit is good-looking. Back in her kitchen, Bri and I had talked at length about how she'd been trying to get him to commit to a real relationship, and how he'd dodged her at every turn. Turns out there ain't a whole lot of romantic options for a single mom in a town of 2,000 in rural South Dakota.

Not a lot of options for bike repair either. In fact, Bri's garage was the closest thing to a bike shop until Miles City, Montana — 200 miles away — and she didn't have the tool I needed.

I thought about the next 200 miles: scorching desert, constant headwind, 80 miles between towns. And now I had permission to skip it. Not only that, my Peace Corps friend Donna lived in Miles City and offered to let me stay as long as it took to fix my bike. It was like waking up too sick to go to school on the morning of a big test you were dreading.

Of course, if I hitched those miles, there would be some people who'd cry foul. "You hitchhiked 240 miles of a 5,000-mile bike tour? Doesn't count!" But then again, that kind of person will look for any excuse to try to rob you of your accomplishments. "You didn't go on the Northern Tier! You didn't dip your back tire in the Atlantic Ocean! Doesn't count!"

Whatever. I wasn't doing this to report to a committee, and I'd already biked more than the entire Northern Tier anyway. At the end of the day, I didn't want to severely screw up my bike in the actual middle of nowhere.

If only conversation with Bruce was as easy as this decision. I gave up and stared out the window in a way I hoped looked contemplative.

*

The next morning, Bruce and Chad came over for breakfast. Bruce mentioned that he was redeploying with the Navy in a few months. Finally, a conversational foothold!

"Yo, I toured the Coast Guard icebreaker last season in Antarctica, and there were like 100 guys sleeping in one room. Is it like that in the Navy?"

"Oh, there were 180 guys in my berth."

"ARE YOU KIDDING? How do you even sleep? Is it just a symphony of snoring and farts?"

He laughed and shrugged. "You can get used to anything."

"Can I ask you an honest question?"

"Sure?"

"What about sex? Like, do people just get creative with where they do it?"

Without missing a beat, as if he got this question all the time, he said, "Oh yeah. In closets, empty vehicles—"

"Just any nook and cranny?"

"Pun intended?"

"Hiyooooo!"

The conversation continued on like this long enough that Bri and Chad eventually drifted away to do their own thing.

"My friend in the army said they hung up sheets and made little wank palaces for themselves. And if someone's sheet was down, you respected that. Is it like *that* in the Navy?"

"I don't know about wank palaces, but..." He gave me a confiding glance and beckoned me closer. "My friend gave me his iPod full of porn. Like, 'We're all in this together.'"

"Dude, that's a good friend!"

I'm not sure it was what most people would consider sparkling conversation, but we were having a blast. I didn't hit the road until past 11.

"Sorry to see you leave," Bruce told me.

And I walked Lucky to a good spot with a wide shoulder, stuck out my thumb, and hoped like hell I could make it to Miles City by sunset.

*

"I'm only going to the next town over," David warned me. "I was up until 5 a.m. at a bachelor party last night."

"No worries."

He was quiet, so I gently floated the conversation rather than pushing it. Out the window, a group of windmills caught my eye, and I snapped a picture.

"Do you want to see them up close?" David asked.

"What do you mean?"

"My cousin owns this land. I can take you up there."

I turned to look at David, really look at him, and decide if I could trust him. I didn't hide my scrutinizing gaze, and he didn't hide from it.

Windmills are immense up close. The blades rotate around a blank, cycloptic eye, but slowly — almost like they weigh 6 tons each. They make an unearthly whisper when they cleave the air. The sound is pervasive, like an ominous soundtrack.

"This is sage grass," David said, plucking a sprig of it and placing it in my palm. "Smell it."

It smelled dusky and warm. He was bent over again, and came up with a small yellow flower. We walked to the top of a hill, prairie spilling out around us in all directions, underneath a sky so blue it could have been finger paint. He pointed out a small square house. It was his aunt's, he said.

"I bet you know this whole area," I said.

He just looked ahead and smiled.

Back in the truck, he said, "Do you want to see the Enchanted Highway?"

"Uh, YEAH!"

We drove through wheat fields for nearly an hour before the road turned to asphalt again. There were houses and a sidewalk, and then a tall, blue sign with unsteady yellow letters that said:

WELCOME

TO

REGENT

ENCHANTED

HIGHWAY
THE
ROAD
OF
A
N
T
I
C
I
P
A
T
I
O
N

And soon, I was standing in the shade underneath a family of metal partridges. A little farther down the road, there were car-sized grasshoppers. Farther still, a fisherman in a boat riding a two-story tsunami.

These scrap metal statues marked a new life for the little town of Regent. In the 1990s, it was dying — no jobs, no prospects for its 171 residents. So Gary Greff, an artist and the town's music teacher, built these eight statues that led all the way up to the interstate. Tourists driving through would have an incentive to come visit Regent, fill up at the gas station, eat at the restaurant, and stay in the hotel.

See how art can change the world?

Hours after David warned me he could only take me to the next town over, we finally arrived.

"North Dakota is a special place," I said. "Thank you for showing it to me."

He gave a shy shrug and said gruffly, "You're welcome."

When he drove away, I tucked the sage grass and the yellow flower into my bandana and smiled. I could have biked right past everything David showed me and never known it existed. I probably would have resented the day's miles, like they were just an obstacle between me and where I was headed. But instead, I got to enjoy an adventure. And that's okay. This journey didn't have to be the Ultimate Test Of My Physical Endurance. It didn't have to be entirely focused on helping those less fortunate. There was still plenty of work to be done for Represent the Village — my trip to Malawi, college applications, and with any luck, coordinating Friday's visa and airfare to the U.S. For now, the best thing I could do for my cause was to take care of myself.

*

The next person who picked me up kinda gave me the creeps: a sallow older guy who had the vibe of someone who'd been living alone in the woods too long.

The best hitches are the ones where you can let down your defenses in front of a complete stranger, and for the duration of your ride, two humans forget the social code and get real. But you can't do that with everyone, and I got the sense that this guy would interpret my live-righteously-and-love-everyone philosophy as sexual interest. If we crossed the line of talking about sex, there might not be any turning back.

Fortunately for me, he mentioned he was going fishing with his 9-year-old grandson, and I seized onto that detail like it was a big ol jughandle on the rock wall.

"Awww, that's such a fun age!" I gushed. "Does he do any activities at school? It's so nice you go fishing with him! My grampa taught me how to play cribbage, and that's still something special we share."

Nothing kills a guy's boner faster than reminding him he's a grandfather.

And this is another of my favorite things about hitchhiking: the chance to try on different versions of myself. Brooke as a sweet, innocent, effusive gal who loves kids like she's a first-grade teacher? Sure, I'll play that part. Especially if it's a shrewd matter of self-preservation. I imagine it's the same rush an antelope feels when she outruns a lion.

The creep would try to change the subject to something more titillating; I would smile brightly and bring it right back to his grandson. I could tell he thought I was an airhead. Good. There's power in being the only one who knows you're the smartest person in the room.

When we got to the next town, I said, "You know what, it's getting kinda late. I'm gonna stay here and get an early start in the morning."

He insisted on dropping me off at an auto mechanic. "I'm sure he can fix whatever's wrong with your bike," he said in this condescending way, like thank god he came along to save me from my own ineptitude. The place was obviously closed. After he pulled out of sight, I sighed and pushed Lucky up a steep hill to get back to the road.

*

I had gone 25 miles in a 200-mile journey, and I had just enough time to get to Miles City by dark. (Rule #5: Don't hitchhike at night unless you have no other choice.)

The thing about the hitching gods is, you can't want it too bad, and you *can't* get impatient. Remember, you are asking for a gift. If you're grateful when you get a ride, graceful when you don't, and patient while you wait, the hitching gods will have mercy on you if you're ever *really* in a jam.

Besides, I had all my camping gear. That's a pretty cushy worst-case scenario.

I threw my thumb up for this nice, clean truck (you can tell a lot about a person by how they treat their car) and it blew past me... but the sloppy jalopy behind it put on the brakes.

I ran over, joyfully, and made my 10-second assessment:

- Bumper sticker for... sheep shearing? That's a new one.
- Truck: cluttered but not dirty.
- Driver: Pure Montana. Crow's feet, handlebar mustache, cowboy hat, dungarees. The sun glinted off the cross that hung around his neck.

The first things George told me about himself: he has a wife and two sons, and he's a devout Mormon. Not only did this immediately put me at ease, it also opened the door to one of my favorite conversations: comparing spiritual beliefs!

Talking openly about religion is taboo in America, right? But I think the reason people avoid these conversations is because they're afraid the other person will attack their beliefs... which is absolutely a rude thing to do. But if you're curious, polite, and interested, and if you focus on parallels and not differences, you can come to some satisfying common ground. And isn't that the entire point of religion, to help people get along with each other?

George told me a story I could relate to:

"I had anger problems when I was younger... especially with my sons. We were workin in the woods one day, and I let my frustration get the best of me. They made a mistake, somethin I can't even remember, and I laid into them, hollerin that they didn't know what the eff they were doin. So I stormed off by myself into the woods, and chopped away at this tree. Well, it fell wrong. It landed on my ankle and broke it. I was trapped."

"Whoa!"

"It was humblin," he said. "I had to call to my sons for help, had to lean on them as they carried me out of the woods. That was the turnin point for me, when I realized I had to get my temper under control. They helped me even though I'd been unfair to them."

"That's the power of kindness."

"That's the power of God."

We got to Donna's apartment as the sun was setting. He wished me luck, gave me his phone number in case I ever needed help, and pulled away. As soon as his car was gone, another one took its spot, and my friend Donna shot out of the passenger seat like a cannonball.

"OMIGOSH BROOKIE YAYYYYYYYYYYYYY!" she squealed, and hit me with a bodylock of a hug.

For the first time in hundreds and hundreds of miles, I felt like I was home.

*

Donna is Dorothy from the *Wizard of Oz* as portrayed by Dolly Parton. Small-town Montana girl, doesn't know she's a total bombshell, first person in her family to leave the country, forever getting tipsy and doing cartwheels. If you asked me when I first met her, I would have told you she couldn't hack it in the Peace Corps. Her own brother bet her $100 she wouldn't last a year. When she did, he said, "Double or nothing."

"He still owes me that $200!" Donna exclaimed when she told me this story.

Donna is one of those rare people who can love completely. Consequently, I heard a lot of heartbreak stories. I listened, of course, but in my chest beats the heart of a crusty cynic, and my deepest inner self thought she was foolish, giving her heart away like that instead of keeping it behind layers of brick and steel and bulletproof glass.

But now I know the truth. You think riding a bike across the country is brave? Try trusting someone after you've been hurt.

Which is exactly what she did. Whirlwind romance, December wedding, and Donna and Adam celebrated the anniversary of their first date as a married couple. The crusty old warden of my heart crossed her arms and scowled and thought, "Gimme 10 minutes with this guy so I can vet him and make sure he's good enough for my friend."

Turns out I didn't need that long. After Donna hit me like a missile, Adam got out of the driver's seat. He had soft eyes and a gentle smile, and his energy was like... like sitting in your favorite seat in your favorite coffee shop and taking your first sip of a chai latte.

"You must be Brooke," he said. "I've heard so much about you."

The crusty old warden of my heart uncrossed her arms and announced, "He's perfect!"

*

The next day, I pushed Lucky to Pedal Power Sports, the only bike shop for hundreds of miles in either direction... and found a handwritten sign on the door saying it was closed. Fortunately, it also gave a phone number, in case of emergency.

20 minutes later, I met Miles.

Miles is the typical tortured genius who's spent his life wrenching in a local bike shop: a mad scientist with a sailor's mouth; half MacGuyver, half Belle's father from *Beauty & the Beast*, and what the hell, half the Beast too.

He rolled in like a thunderstorm, gave me and Lucky a skeptical glare, and skipped the pleasantries. "All right lady, what's so important I had to come in on my day off? That's a joke. This your bike? You said the bottom bracket's fucked?"

He hoisted Lucky up, clamped her into the repair stand, and started work; it broke my heart a little, to see her hanging there so helpless, here in the bike equivalent of the emergency room.

"I don't know what to tell ya, lady, I don't know if I can fix this thing," he grunted, yanking on a spanner wrench. "I've never seen a bottom bracket like this, and it could take weeks for the part to come in. The only thing I can think... and I ain't makin you a promise or nothin, but... Joey had a bike in here last week..." He rose and started rummaging on a shelf, through bins of greasy parts. "... and I think he took out a bottom bracket that might work – MIGHT, mind you, if I can find it in this shithole... AHA!" He extracted a part that looked like a spool of thread, wiped it off, and came back to my bike.

I just smiled and wrote down everything he said.

---

things miles said while he fixed lucky

"If this mother tightens in, I'm going to shit."

"This bitch has no threads."

"If this works, I'm gonna shit."

"If this works, woman, you're the luckiest woman this side of hell."

"I'm getting closer... that's what she said."

"Mother *goose*... This is gonna be the goddamndest thing I've ever put together."

"If this sonofabitch gets together, you're gonna piss your pants lady."

"You've gotta be shitting me. You have *got* to be shitting me."

"We'll see if we can give her the good and tight business... We have got the guttentight. That's some German."

"Now, if I can remember how to get these bastards back in the right holes..."

To his surprise (but not to mine), the part worked.

"God's lookin out for you. I don't know what to tell you, honey," he said, shaking his head. "We're gonna write this in the book."

"What book?" I asked.

"The book of OH SHIT."

I laughed, and Miles gave Lucky's pedals a spin. No creak, no wobble. Solid, ready for the next 1,500 miles, or hell, another 4,000. My girl Lucky.

He refused to accept my money, just gave me his card with his phone number and told me to call him anytime I needed him, because I was a guest in his state, and even though some people might not think it's a big deal, god dammit it is. As I embarked with a newfound sense of hope and belief in the kindness of my fellow man, he looked at me and said, "I cannot believe, woman, how lucky you are."

"Thanks, Miles."

"Now if you tell anyone I fixed this, don't tell em."

Sorry Miles.

*

I was entering the punishing portion of my cross-country bike tour: long stretches between towns and, by extension, water sources. And we weren't even in the mountains yet! Further west, I would face 3,000-foot elevation gains in grizzly and cougar country.

In an effort to avoid biking on the interstate, I pointed Lucky's handlebars west, across the Yellowstone River, and along a network of country roads lazily spanning vast, flat fields. Usually I'm stirred by a landscape untouched by humanity. But out here, where the land and the sky stretched out past forever, I felt more intimidation than inspiration. After 20 soggy gravel miles, the road finally turned to tarmac again and I let out a triumphant "WOOOOOOO!" You'll never know it's possible to love pavement until you bike 20 miles through the mud.

From there, it was an easy 19 miles to the town of Forsyth: population 1,800, a sliver of civilization where Donna's mom was kind enough to make up the guest room for me. Even better, it was the night of the Fourth of July Potluck in the neighboring town of Rosebud!

"It's totally lame!" Donna said apologetically. "But my mom will be there, and Adam's whole family. And there'll be fireworks!"

"Are you kidding? That sounds awesome!"

It was. The Rosebud Music Hall had been cleared out to make room for long folding tables heaped with homemade Fourth of July food: hot dogs, hamburgers, grilled chicken, potato salad, macaroni salad, chips, watermelon, cookies, brownies, and jello, all of it tastefully arranged inside inflatable kiddie pools. It was a cross-country cyclist's dream. I ate two heaping plates and shared adventure stories with Adam's family.

When it got dark, we set up lawn chairs in the middle of the street and enjoyed the fireworks display. Donna's littlest niece, Alaina, insisted on sitting next to me, and entertained me with her running commentary on the fireworks. "THAT one was the BIGGEST! No, THAT ONE! That one's the BIGGEST biggest!"

It was cold enough that we were wrapped in blankets, and Alaina asked to trade with me. After the deal was done, she whispered, "It has bird poop on it." Before I could protest, a firework exploded overhead and she said, "You have sparkles in your glasses!"

"Yep!" I said. "The fireworks sprinkled down and got caught inside them!"

"REALLY?!"

I shrugged. "Why not?"

*

In eastern Montana, sometimes there were 50 miles between towns, and some of the towns consisted of a few houses and maybe a church or a bar or a post office. I alternated between weary and inspired. I saw antelopes and mule deer and an immense sky splashed with cirrus clouds. I saw vast meadows hemmed in by crooked barbed-wire fences, sage grass and stratified rock formations and a road sign promising Helena was 300 miles away.

There were times when the only sign of humanity was the road stretching out ahead. There were times I was so happy that I yelled at the top of my lungs, "I LOVE THIS!!!"

It was beautiful, in the way that something huge and forbidding can be beautiful, in the way it reminds you that your life is a quite fragile thing.

Melstone, Mont.
93 days · 4,217 miles

I sat still and straight with a calm smile on my face.

Luke's eyes were bulging and flecks of spittle flew from his lips as he yelled. His entire body was an exclamation point, and he jabbed his finger in the air like he was trying to pop it. Outside there were the sounds of muffled explosions.

"The sacrifices I MADE for MY COUNTRY — I shed BLOOD for my country." His teeth were bared. "And these people who don't love our country, I would love to line em up and SHOOT em all, personally."

"I feel your frustration," I said.

"Damn RIGHT I'm frustrated! I help EVERYONE. I give until it HURTS. I mean, I helped you — you asked me for help, and I was like... well hey, listen, I got a room in my trailer."

"I know. And I appreciate it so much."

"But that's just how I was RAISED. You gotta GIVE until you BLEED."

"If more people were that generous, the world would be a better place."

He scowled at me and let a pause gather like a water droplet. Then he said, deliberately, "You really are an attractive woman."

"Thank you, Luke," I said. "That's always nice to hear."

He scowled. More explosions outside. The fireworks show felt like it had been going on forever. He got on another rant, about Obama and the color of his skin.

Seven hours earlier, in broad daylight at the picnic table outside the bar, his stories were jocular. He had just moved to town, bought a tract of land where he was going to build his dream house and a little cabin for his aging father. Plenty of room to hunt and for his dogs to roam. A place where he could just be alone. For now he was living in a trailer, and I was welcome to stay there for the night if I didn't want to camp out.

"I ain't a pervert or nothin," he told me.

He said he'd been sober for more than a decade, and the bartender, a woman a little older than my mom, vouched for him. He seemed harmless. Just one of those guys who thinks his life is a movie, who views himself as Han Solo: the lovable, roguish lone wolf who does things his way.

Luke (laughing): So I did, I put my gun to his head —

Me (playing along, mock shock): Luke, you did not!

Luke: An' then I turn to the sheriff, an' I says, "Can I kill im?"

Me (chiding): And what did the sheriff say to that?

Luke (like a teacher affectionately rebuking a favorite student): No, Luke, ya can't kill im... but only because it's against the law.

Luke (as himself): Pleeeeeeeeeeeeeeease?

The stories were claptrap, of course, exaggerated to the point of fiction. Like a letter you've read so many times it's worn soft as fabric.

206

But the character of his stories changed here in his house, at 10:30 at night with fireworks exploding outside. This is where he would keep his guns.

He had a trailer out front where my bike was locked up. When he threw open the doors, I heard frantic scratching. He had two dogs, bloodhounds, in cages not bigger than their bodies. They couldn't even turn around. They were whining, scratching at the doors, their tails wagging desperately, like wretched villagers supplicating themselves before an angry god. He turned off the light, and they became more frantic, whimpering but not barking, as if they knew better than to bark. He closed the door, slicing the sunlight thinner and thinner until the door boomed closed and there was only the sound of their claws scrabbling at the bars of their cages.

I thought about his father, his elderly father.

Luke was telling the same story he'd told me before. Only now his voice was lowered, tense.

"So I did, I put my gun to his head. And then I turn to the sheriff and I says, 'Can I kill im?'

'No, Luke, ya can't kill im.'

…

'Please?'"

And that is when I saw how this could go very badly for me.

I hear his footsteps coming down the hall,
see the door push open, his silhouette.
I feel the cold barrel of the gun against my head
as he tells me what I am going to do
to keep him from pulling the trigger.

Here is what I did:

I sat still and straight with a calm smile on my face. I said things like, "I feel your frustration." Inside, my mind was running the calculations.

The facts: Everyone in town knows I'm here. The next house is so close you could touch it; if I scream, they'll hear. If he shoots me, they'll hear. I told the bar owners I'd eat breakfast there. My family knows I'm here.

I think the fireworks triggered some PTSD. If he comes into my room, I'll say, "If you touch me, I'll scream. If you leave me alone, I'll never tell anyone. If you kill me, you will go to jail. Think about your land."

Or I could escape right now. Say I need to go to the bar to use the wifi. "My dad gets all worried if I don't text him every night. He just loves me. You're a dad, you understand." I'll knock on doors until I find the bartender and ask if I can sleep on her couch.

But... Luke is new in this town. What would that do to his reputation? I understand that this is self-preservation, but the stakes are high on his end, too. This is a new start for him. Don't ruin his entire life unless you genuinely think he's going to ruin yours. We'll call this... an experiment in trust.

That was what decided it. He had too much at stake — his land, his dad, his dogs, his freedom — to risk it on me.

I sat still and straight with a calm smile on my face.

I spoke gently, trying to channel the conversation toward calmer territory. Don't let him lay in his bed stewing. I never got him to calm, but I got him to calmer, and that was as close as he was gonna get.

"Well Luke, it's getting late. But hey. I'm really grateful I met you. It's a scary world out there, and it means a lot to have a safe place to sleep."

*

my door didn't close all the way.

i slept with my feet to the door, and kept my bear spray under my pillow all night.

i prayed.

the walls were paper thin.

every time he rolled over, i froze and listened for his footstep.
when i did fall asleep, i dreamt i was in this room
listening.

*

I surprised myself by waking up after 7. I heard Luke in the kitchen.

I sighed. *See, he was never gonna hurt me. He's a good guy after all.*

At the bar, over breakfast, Luke got worked up again and started yelling his invectives. I half-listened, let the other patrons take some of the heat. Don't worry you guys, he just gets this way sometimes.

*

Later that day, with miles between us, I started to construct the narrative of what happened.

I spent the night in a strange man's house. He had a panic attack, a moment of PTSD, but he was harmless, I thought, resigned. *Lesson learned: You can trust people.*

I felt sludgy, like I was caught in a tedious dream, but my muscle fibers twitched like they were being electrocuted by all the coffee in my bloodstream. My stomach hurt.

Pushing up the last long hill before LaVina, I heard a car honk at me. I turned my head in time to see a girl with long, blonde hair smiling and waving. *Is that Cat?* I thought.

I knew she lived somewhat near this area of Montana; I was going to visit her in a couple days. Maybe she had gone to a city nearby or something, maybe she would stop and I could talk to her, god that would be nice, to talk to a fucking *friend* right now, to someone who understood me and who could empathize with the rough fucking night I just weathered.

But the car didn't slow. It just dwindled into the distance until it winked out of existence.

I burst into hysterical sobs.

It was like a storm that blankets a windshield in rain. I had to pull over. There was a dirt road, Emory Road, that spurred off to the right. I remember the name because Emory is where I went to college, and I cried a lot there too.

I pulled over and slumped over the handlebars and let the sobs wrack my body. A few cars passed by. No one stopped; no one even slowed. Maybe a cyclist having a nervous breakdown on the side of the road is just part of the landscape of Montana.

I didn't try to stop it, just felt it and let it flow. I had constructed a lie. The lesson here wasn't some platitude about trust. The lesson was that I had to listen to my gut, that I couldn't sacrifice myself for the sake of politeness. Worst-case scenario, that man could have hurt me badly. Best-case scenario, I biked 80 miles on a few hours of spotty sleep, and *I felt like shit.*

I was so alone. There was no one I could call, no one I could talk to. Just me and my bike in the whole wide world. So I stroked Lucky's handlebars — it's okay girl, I'm gonna be okay — and then wrapped my arms around myself in a pitiful, dejected hug.

*

That night I slept in a park, and when I woke up at 4:15, I decided to just go.

Early in the morning, the sky looks two-dimensional, like dry black construction paper. To the east, a haze of light sifts up like smoke. Before me, the obsidian shadows of mountains. Beside me, great rolling hills furred over with long grass, like the backs of sleeping bears. The air is moist with dew and fragrant with the smell of growing plants; the headwind dances light and playful. I breathe it in and close my eyes and smile. In a few hours, the sun will scorch the air until it's dry as a spent ember, and the grass will ripple in the howling headwind, so I squeeze all the joy that I can out of these miles.

In this moment, the boundary between me and the landscape blurs. I am a point of motion within this shadowy stillness of 4-something a.m. I am connected by my breath to my surroundings. How lucky I am to get to be a part of wild Montana for this single splendid moment.

As the sun shines and the day wakes up and the cars regain control of the road, I take a break.

What is freedom?

Sitting on the sidewalk and leaning against the wall of a gas station, eating brown sugar cinnamon Pop Tarts and gas station coffee for breakfast.

*

I lingered too long in a café called CAFÉ, and longer still in the Harlowtown library tying up loose ends for Represent the Village. There were follow-up emails to send to schools, updates to post on social media, and thank-you notes to write to donors. Over the course of my trip, I'd managed to raise $3,440 — enough to send each of my students to college in Malawi for at least a year.

I walked out of the crisp, invigorating AC into air so hot it felt like I was wading through it. The sky was a cruel, cloudless blue. Time for an executive decision: For the remaining 37 miles, every time I found shade, I would take a break and drink water.

I took three breaks all day.

Break #1

A shadow about as wide as an end table cast by an informational sign for The Crazy Mountains. It was so small I couldn't even sit, so I stood and regarded the ridgeline falling in wrinkles like metatarsals, gray and mottled with spots of trees and stripes of snow. According to the sign, the Crows call them Awaxaawippiia and consider them a site of spiritual refuge and vision quests. Settlers named them the Crazy Mountains after a woman lost her family in the journey west and ran off to die or maybe live there[23].

I thought about her, looking at those mountains. Why'd she go up there? Was it really just to die? Was it in search of a vision? Or was it an assertion of freedom? Maybe she gave in to that low, velvet voice that emerges from the shadows of your brain when you're standing at the edge of something tall, to say one soft word: "Jump."

Does that make her crazy? Or brave?

Break #2

Chatted with a geologist under some trees in his yard while peacocks screamed from just beyond the picket fence.

Break #3

I leaned against the side of a barn in a thin strip of shade and sipped water gone hot. A truck pulled up, and a guy around my age got out. He had sandy hair and ruddy cheeks, and greeted me with a smile and a "Hullo!"

"Hey!" I said. "I was just resting in the shade, but I'm about to get going."

"Are you sure? It's cooler in the barn," he said. His words sounded heavy, like they were slipping back down his throat. "Do you drink Paepsi?"

"Paepsi?"

"Pop?"

"Oh, sure!" I said and followed him inside. He introduced himself as Ned.

"Nice to meet you, Ned! Your accent is so interesting — where are you from?"

"Here!" he laughed. "I'm a hud-right."

---

[23] Writer Mark Melroy asserts that this is probably just a myth. According to his research, when the Crows said "vision quest," early white settlers heard "psychotic break" and the name "Crazy Mountains" was born.

"Sorry?"

"A Hutterite! Do you know the Mennonites, the Amish? Like that. I'm a Hutterite."

Instantly, I became self-conscious about how I was dressed, but Ned seemed unfazed. He gave me a Diet Sunkist from the fridge. "I'm a cow-man," he said, and pulled aside a curtain in the corner of the room to show me a small bunk where he sleeps during the calving season. "You're welcome to take a nap if you want."

The door opened, and a round man with a white beard and a wisp of white hair on his head walked in. With him was a little girl in homemade clothes, blonde hair peeking out from a black-and-white polka-dot headscarf.

"Hullo Paul," Ned said. "Hullo Sadie."

Paul didn't seem off-put to find Ned hanging out with a strange woman in a short dress with her knees and shoulders showing. In fact, when he heard I was riding my bike across the country, he insisted on heading back to his house to bring me some food. He returned with his wife Mary — a stout, strong woman with round glasses — and Sadie's older brother Jacob. Mary gave me a plastic grocery bag of store-bought dinner rolls and frozen cold cuts and yellow American cheese. Sadie gave me a Diet Sunkist.

"Has anyone tried to kill you?" Paul asked.

I asked them about their family. Mary said they have seven children, three of them sons. "Daughters bring nothing but heartache," she said, looking down at her hands and shaking her head.

I glanced at little Sadie, who stared back at me like I was an alien, or possibly the coolest person she had ever met. I hoped, selfishly perhaps, that she would get to do whatever she wanted with her life.

"You're big," Jacob said. "Do you have a car?"

"Nope."

"Do you have a *house*?" asked Sadie.

"No house," I said, smiling.

She looked confused. "Where do you *live*?"

"Do you know where Antarctica is?" I asked.

"She doesn't know anything!" Paul volunteered cheerfully.

"I live at the bottom of the world," I told her.

And when I said goodbye, I found that the sky had sprouted a crop of fluffy little clouds and the wind had shifted to my back.

*

That evening, I found myself at a bar called the Checkerboard Inn. The light hung in the air like chalkdust and the walls were covered with dollar bills. There had to be thousands of them, missives from all the travelers who'd found themselves in this little place over the years; a small fortune written over with names and dates and drawings and private jokes. I rummaged in my wallet and came up with a dollar, wrote a love letter to someone who'll never read it, and taped it up with the others.

The door opened, letting in a beam of dazzling sunlight, and a man took the seat next to me. He reminded me of an old pickup truck: scarred but solid, with a low rumble of a voice and hard lines around his eyes. Not as strong as he may have once been, but tough as ever.

He sipped Heineken from a bottle and told me about his years working in a coal mine. I asked about light and fresh air and canaries; he spoke of portable oxygen and lights the color of cheap beer lining the tunnels. He told me about longwall miners that slice coal like lunchmeat, and continuous miners — machines that grind out whole rooms, hallways wide enough to drive through, like parking garages beneath the earth, destined only to collapse. He talked about coal dust, how it coats your skin and gathers in the wrinkles on your face and hides beneath your fingernails and inside your lungs. In his low, rumbling voice, he painted me a picture of a world that exists underground, where men toil in the dark and the cold to bring heat and light to the world above.

Naturally, the conversation wandered over to dwindling coal jobs and the rise of green energy; you can imagine where he stood on that topic. As he spoke, I worked the mental calculations on how to respectfully phrase my dissenting opinion. Until he heaved a deep sigh, like he was shifting into low gear, and said, "A lot of people say coal is evil, but... it gave me a job, and my son and my nephew too." He met my gaze. "How can something be evil if it supported my entire family?"

His eyes snagged me. They were clear and gray, the color of scuffed and faded concrete, those hard lines radiating from the edges. From squinting in the dim light of the mines, from squinting in the sunlight upon his return to the surface, and squinting now, here in this bar. Squinting, I realized, was how he must have taught himself to not cry.

How perfectly fucked up, that our men must teach themselves how not to cry.

This wasn't a conversation about pollution or the environment. He and his family loved this place, and coal was the only good job here, and now the coal companies were pulling out and his family was struggling and the future was uncertain. He was witnessing the death of his culture, and he was afraid.

There wasn't a damn thing I could do to help him, but I could listen. So there among the dollar bills I did just that[24], and

---

[24] For the record, he didn't change my mind. I believe in sustainable energy, in harnessing the tremendous power of wind and sunlight, but I also believe that innovation need not come at the cost of a dignified life for a man like this one.

let his words fall on my mind like raindrops on scuffed and faded concrete.

diner break: snook's diner
(white sulphur springs, mont.)

A fluffy omelet filled with sharp cheddar and bright chunks of bell pepper and tomatoes and onion, sprinkled with good salt and freshly ground pepper, with a side of field greens and homemade bread and strong coffee.

After days of travel across an arid desert, through towns where the only business is a bar, when you're physically exhausted and you haven't had a good night's sleep in days, when you're body is sputtering along on gas station coffee and Pop Tarts, this place is an oasis.

No trees, no shade, just that angry Montana sun baking the land and any bikers hapless enough to traverse it. Up ahead, a rusty gate across a dirt road branching off to the right. As good a place to rest as any.

I leaned Lucky against the gate and sat in the little splash of shade she gave me. The wind was strong, but I felt safe and loved, there in the shadow of my trusty bike. I gazed at the down tube, at the tea fortune I taped there thousands of miles ago.

Live righteously and love everyone.

Man, yeah it's a corny tea fortune, but wouldn't the world be a better place if we all made this promise?

*

Big ol hill coming out of town, and a headwind that met me at every curve. It felt like I was pedaling through pudding, but I dug deep and found the joy in it. Turns out strength isn't gritting your teeth and forcing your way through; it's finding your smile even when your muscles are shaking.

When I finally got to the top, I let out a wild howl and punched the air.

"BROOKE! MOTHAFUCKIN! **MARSHALL!!**" I screamed.

Emboldened by my victory, I decided to see if I could borrow some shade. Just up ahead, I spied a lanky, stoop-shouldered guy pushing a lawnmower out of his garage.

"Excuse me," I said. "Would you mind if I sat in the shadow of your garage to cool off? I just biked up that hill, and it was a doozy."

And of course the answer was no, I had to sit in a chair, and would I like a beer? Before long, I was sipping a cold soda and eating chicken with Mel and his wife Wanda — one of those impeccably coiffed women who's been 39 for years. Their mini Australian shepherd Stormy chased a ball I threw, and they insisted I stay for a barbecue they were having and pitch a tent in their yard.

It was tempting, but I was a slave to my deadline, so I thanked them for their hospitality and hit the road.

And then the ride became EPIC.

Suddenly, out of nowhere, there were TREES. A whole pine forest! I laughed with delight: After days and days in the desert, I can't tell you how excited I was to see TREES again! The road abruptly pitched downward, twisting and snaking like an electrified wire, through this lush timberland of jagged, viridescent arrowheads pointing toward the cloudless sky.

I shot around the curves of asphalt smooth and silver as cadmium, scored with twin lines of daffodil, the landscape slowly rising higher around me. Occasionally a car would pass; I felt so sorry for the people inside. They were craning their necks to look at this magnificent place. They were one step removed, observing it through a chunky, ugly viewfinder. I was *in it*. I was breathing in the scent of pine needles and soaking up the sunlight and feeling the wind dry the sweat on my skin as I bombed down a hill I had fought with all my strength to get up.

And then, as the land flattened out and I resumed pedaling, I glanced up at the horizon to see a range of enormous mountains rearing up in front of me.

"Well shit," I said aloud, equal parts giddy and terrified. "I gotta climb you, don't I."

*

"You know there's some mountains up ahead, don't you?"

It was a question usually asked with a scowl by some old dude in a gas station. What I wanted to say was, "Uh, yeah dude. We're in Montana. It's kind of in the name."

What I actually said was, "Yep! I've come this far, I can make it all the way."

I figured it wasn't personal, but when enough people question whether you can do something, it starts to get in your head. Maybe they know something you don't. So even though I was energized by my epic ride into Helena, I still felt frayed and stretched almost to a breaking point.

Fortunately, my Warm Showers host was understanding and basically let me go to bed at 5 p.m. The next morning, over a breakfast of eggs, field greens, and whole-grain toast, she told me about her bike advocacy work in Montana. Then she asked if I wanted a chicken-salad sandwich for the road. When I hesitated, she gave me a little smile and made it for me.

Maybe angels *are* real.

Armed with that sandwich, a couple bottles of water, and a playlist consisting of equal parts Jay-Z and Jimmy Buffet, I set out to face my first Montana montaña: MacDonald Pass, elevation 6,312 feet, a 2,000-foot climb over 9.8 miles.

As soon as I got to the foot of the mountain, I laughed at myself. Hang on a second, I've done this before! This is just like the hills on the east coast, only longer and not as steep.

You know how you get up a mountain? You put your bike in low gear and take it easy. You find the rhythm of your breath. You stop in the shade if you get hot. You eat half of a chicken salad sandwich when you need some slow-burning energy. You drink lots of water. Sure, you're tired, but it's easier to just keep going than to stop and have to start back up again. So you dig deep and find your aquifer of strength.

The trees start to thin out. There's more sun up here. You glance to your left and are startled to see an enormous landscape yawning up at you.

You round a long curve and see a sign warning trucks to shift into low gear.

I don't care how bad your legs are burning, as soon as you see the summit, you *float* the rest of the way. And then you thrust your fist high into the air, because you're a badass amazon and those gas station assholes don't know what they're talking about.

And then, in 15 giddy minutes, you glide down the other side of a mountain you just spent 2 ½ hours climbing.

*

It's always a bit of a rude awakening when you have to start pedaling again. Fortunately, I spied a little wooden general store up ahead. I was up the driveway and leaning my bike against the wall faster than you can say "ice cream break."

A couple dudes in motorcycle gear were sitting on the bench outside. "Room for one more?" I asked, and sat down before they could respond. As I devoured the rest of my chicken salad sandwich, one of the guys took out a map and asked about my route. The other one pulled off his helmet and turned to me with a smile. He had crystal blue eyes and rosy cheeks and messy blond hair. "I'm Jack," he said.

"What do you do for work, Jack?"

"Diesel engine mechanic back in Helena."

"Oh, like on 18-wheelers?" I said around a mouthful of ice cream. "I used to drive those."

Ladies, it never gets old seeing a guy's eyes widen when you tell him you can drive a big rig. Jack's buddy, perhaps realizing there was no room for third wheels in bicycling, motorcycling, or whatever the hell was going on here, gracefully excused himself. Not that I had any illusions that this cute motorcycle cowboy in his 20s was all that interested in Ol Meemaw Brooke. It was just a fun conversation... like, a two-hour-long fun conversation!

I had to get going if I was going to make it to that evening's destination: Ovando. Sitting at the confluence of the Great Divide Mountain Bike Route and the Lewis & Clark Bicycle Trail, Ovando is a mecca of sorts for bike tourists. Maybe I'd meet some other bikers and spend the night sitting around a campfire telling stories and feeling like a part of a community.

"Well, listen, if you need to fill up your water bottles, you should meet me at my dad's ranch," Jack said hastily as I got up. "It's 15 miles down the road."

Hey, I'll take any opportunity to not have to haul as much water. He gave me directions and roared away.

It was a warm Montana summer day. Rolling fields and cattle that raised their heads to stare at me blankly as I passed. Pine forests and a couple biking from Canada to Mexico with their infant son. 15 miles later, I saw Jack's purple motorcycle parked in front of a farmhouse and pulled over. Before I knew it, we'd spent another hour strolling around his property. We went inside to fill my water bottles, and he offered me a beer.

"Nah, I gotta stay straight if I'm gonna make it to Ovando."

"I'd be happy to give you a ride. I can just borrow my dad's truck."

As if on cue, Jack Senior walked in. He regarded the sweaty stranger in his kitchen with bland interest, and cracked a Bud Light Lime as Jack introduced me.

He frowned at his son. "Jack, you're gonna let this gal bike all the way to Ovando and not offer her a ride? I thought I taught you manners."

"I tried, she doesn't want it!"

"Hitchhiking kinda defeats the purpose of *biking* across the country," I pointed out.

"How far have you gone?" Jack Senior asked me.

"4,500 miles..."

"4,500 miles," he said, satisfied. "So if you hitch 30, does that really make a difference?"

Jack looked at me hopefully. I smiled and rolled my eyes. "Come on Jack, you heard the man."

*

Cyclists passing through Ovando can camp outside, or for a $5 donation, they can stay in a teepee, a sheep wagon, or an old prison. As I pondered this decision, the woman at the welcome center said, "Don't forget to get your picture taken by the camera outside! These grizzlies sure didn't!" And then she showed me a picture of two grizzly bears who had wandered through town only a few nights before.

Come to think of it, the sheep wagon looked a bit sturdier than the teepee.

Jack took me to a bar called Trixi's. I'd describe the motif as "dead animal heads galore" and the hamburgers as "gigantic." I beat Jack at a game of Ms. Pac Man, ate a hamburger and all my fries and some of his too, and downed a pint of cider. Our knees kept bumping under the bar.

And then he drove me back to my sheep wagon. He put the truck in park. The rich golden light of the setting sun illuminated his long, blond eyelashes.

"You have beautiful eyelashes," I said.

"Aww shucks, this ugly face?"

"I think you're pretty cute," I said, smiling at him.

"Really?" he said softly. "I think you're pretty cute too..."

We gazed at each other in the warm, syrupy evening light...

` ... and then I blurted out, "Uh, well, thanks for the ride!" and basically leaped out of the truck.

Jack looked a little confused, but smiled and gave me a hesitant wave and drove out of sight. I stood alone in the parking lot and watched the dust from his truck settle. *Ha-ha... huh... oh well...*

I turned to walk away, stepped in the shallowest pothole in the universe, and promptly sprained my ankle.

Oh fuck I broke my ankle, was my first thought as I lay on the ground. But then Maple took the wheel.

Okay, Dr. Brooke, let's not jump to the worst possible outcome. C'mon, let's assess the damage. When the going gets tough, it's good to have a no-nonsense inner adult you can rely on.

I got up and gently poured pressure into my right foot. It was stiff and tender, but it could hold weight. Great news! Next step: limp over to my panniers and locate my first-aid kit.

My first-aid kit consisted of a handful of Ibuprofen in a Ziploc bag. I shrugged, popped a couple, and tied a long sock tight around my ankle. Foot bound and elevated, I made an appointment with Dr. Google. Turns out if you're gonna injure any body part on a bike tour, your ankle is the best you can do. In fact, the motion of pedaling stretches your calf muscles and keeps your ankle from stiffening up. So *really*, if you think about it, biking the last 566 miles to Seattle was the healthiest possible decision I could make.

Sitting there alone outside my sheep wagon, the only biker in a bike town, I laughed at myself and thought, *Sometimes the universe kicks you in the butt because you deserve it. Next time, I'm kissing the cute guy.*

diner break: the stray bullet (ovando, mont.)

I'm a free spirit who traipses after her dreams like a little kid following a butterfly. But I'm also a sweaty bald gal who hobbles around because I've been perched on a hard leather seat and hunched over handlebars for the last eight hours (and I just sprained my ankle!), and did I mention that I've been wearing the same dress every single day for three months?

Needless to say, sometimes I get a little self-conscious when I walk into a diner.

But not at the Stray Bullet. They didn't even blink. Not only was I a totally normal occurrence, I was their *key demographic*. What a privilege it is to live in your freedom and not feel weird about it.

The Garden of One Thousand Buddhas
99 days · 4,566 miles

In a quiet field surrounded by gentle hills, just outside Arlee, you'll find the Garden of One Thousand Buddhas. Arranged in a circle representing the eight-spoked Dharma wheel is a white stone wall. Atop that wall are 1,000 miniature temples; within each of those temples, a tiny stone Buddha.

In the center of the wheel is a massive statue of Yum Chenmo, the Great Mother who represents enlightenment. She wears a beatific smile and a golden crown, on a throne of marigold and forget-me-not and candied fennel.

Other, larger statues dot the garden, on stones and pedestals, among the trees, beside the lake. One of them sits on a rough cut of stone on which is engraved:

You can search throughout the entire universe for someone who is more deserving of your love and affection than you are yourself, and that person is not to be found anywhere. You yourself, as much as anybody in the entire universe, deserve your love and affection.

I gave him my necklace.

*

I spent a rest day with Cat, a friend from McMurdo. Her parents fawned over me; her mother offered me arnica gel and ice packs for my ankle, and her father beamed and told corny jokes. Cat took me on a day trip to Big Fork. I limped along beside her, and we discussed the elements of existence, the meanings of dreams, our favorite tarot cards, which desserts pair best with various hot beverages, and that age-old question: If you *had* to be coated in any condiment, which one would it be and why?

We ended the day sitting on her back porch, watching the sun set over Flathead Lake, picking at homemade scones, and playing with kittens. The next day, I knew, would be the start of my final push. There would be desert and mountains, thirst and fear, pain and exhaustion, and the yawning maw of loneliness.

But for now, at least, I had a friend.

*

I stopped by the Adventure Cycling Association headquarters on my way out of Missoula. I was excited, hoping to maybe make some friends or share a conversation. Alas, it wasn't meant to be. Most of the cyclists there were old dudes shrink-wrapped in bright spandex who were just starting their journey. The one guy my age scowled at me; he gave the impression of someone who was running away.

Who am I kidding? I thought, biking away. *What, I'm gonna make lifelong friends with people who are biking in the opposite direction eight days before I finish my tour?*

Talking to those strangers, trading our routes and listing off the brands of our gear, felt like I was on a script. *Is this really me?* I thought. *What is a human without connections? Am I even real?*

Within the first mile, I got a flat tire.

Fixing a flat isn't difficult, but it is a pain in the ass. If it's your front tire, it's relatively easy, because you don't have to deal with the bike chain.

But come on, it's never your front tire.

So you pull aside the chain (it nips you for your trouble) and pry the tire off with your tire lever (it pinches you for your trouble). If you have a spare tube, you just throw that sucker on and inflate it and go on your merry way. If you don't, you must play the most awful game: Find That Puncture. It's easy if you have a bucket of water, but who carries a bucket of water on a bike tour?

Using a teeny tiny hand pump, you inflate the tube until it's bloated like a boiled hot dog, and then hold it next to your face and try to feel the wind or hear the faint "squeeeeeeee" of escaping air over the sound of traffic. When you finally find it, the puncture is almost invisible, seemingly insignificant, a tiny wound with the power to bring down an entire bicycle.

When I got my first flat in that fateful three days, it just so happened I was across the road from an auto body shop in the middle of nowhere. This was fortunate, because the twisted little shred of metal embedded in my tire wasn't coming out. I popped inside, borrowed a pair of needle-nosed pliers, and fixed the flat.

When I got another flat the next morning, I was frustrated. And when I got yet another flat that afternoon, I freaked out and sobbed.

The next day…

I was in the breakdown lane of I-90, coasting down a hill and feeling pretty good about the miles I was putting in, when I felt that telltale wobble and heard the slopping noise a tire makes when the tube loses pressure.

No. You have got to be fucking kidding me.

I pulled over to the guardrail. My entire body was tense, from the soles of my feet to the crown of my head. I was shaking with rage. I wanted to hurl Lucky in front of the next semi truck and throw myself into traffic just to end this fucking nightmare.

Fuck this place, fuck this bike, fuck this tour, fuck you, fuck me, fuck everything, FUCK FUCK FUCK FUCK FUCK.

And then Fiddlehead put a gentle hand on Maple's clenched fist.

Okay, she said with a little smile.

You have a flat tire. This is frustrating, and it will slow you down. But there is a solution to this problem, and yes, it's tedious, but freaking out is only going to make it take longer. So let's sing a song.

Ugh. I hate it when she's right.

Cars and trucks and semis hurtled past as I sang myself a little bubble of peace and remembered: Oh yeah, I actually kind of

patching a flat on the side of the interstate playlist
"No Woman, No Cry"
"The Gash"
"The Spiderbite Song"
"Rocky Raccoon"

like patching flats. Sure, it's not as fun as actually *riding* a bike, but it's satisfying. I felt a little pang of guilt for my reproach toward Lucky. She was the victim here. She let me ride on her back across the whole entire country — it's the least I could do to remove a thorn from her paw.

My composure lasted all of six miles, when I found myself once again sitting on the guardrail and sobbing. I had two choices:

   a. 21 miles on an all-uphill "bike path" that was actually a forest service road pocked with potholes and ruts and strewn with softball-sized rocks, or
   b. 21 miles, all uphill, on the interstate

"**FUCK!!!!!!!! THIS!!!!!!!!!!!**" I screamed out into harsh, unfeeling Montana. There was no response, just the drone of cars on the interstate. How I hated them, each and every individual one of them. All those lucky fucks enjoying A/C and letting a robot carry them up this mountain.

I was catatonic, tears leaking out of my dead and staring eyes. I didn't want to make a decision. There was no right decision. Both options sucked. This was my reality, and the longer I sat crying on this guardrail, the longer I had to exist in it.

With a sharp breath, I screamed, "**FUCK!!!!!!!!!!!! MONTANA!!!!!!!**" at the top of my lungs.

And then I got up and resigned myself to 21 miles uphill on the interstate.

*

An animal caged might pace the floor, or sit in one place rocking back and forth. It might sleep all day or bang its head or bite itself, drawing blood.

Why is it doing this?

This behavior — stereotypic behavior, it's called — is a natural reaction to an unnatural situation. The cage is to blame. The enclosure at the zoo or the bare walls of a research laboratory, after all, are a poor substitute for the kind of environment a monkey or parrot might call home.

And so the monkey rocks back and forth, back and forth, back and forth. It hunches in a corner and rocks back and forth and tugs at its ears. The parrot grooms itself with single-minded obsession. It digs its beak deeper and deeper, pulling out its feathers in bloody clumps.

You see the same behavior in people, too. Prisoners cut themselves, swallow sharp objects, bang their heads against the wall. Old folks with dementia in nursing homes pinch, scratch, hit, bite, and burn themselves, punch objects, pull their hair.

Institutionalized mentally ill patients bite themselves, press their eyeballs, and bang their heads against hard surfaces.

In a cage, self-destruction becomes your only means of self-determination. Or, to put it another way: If you can't get out of your cage, you might go out of your mind.

Struggling uphill along a breakdown lane on the verge of tears, pummeled by fumes carried on a hot headwind, feeling like I'm biking through dirty bathwater, the only thought on my mind is: Why the fuck am I doing this?

Because for all the suffering in this moment, at least I'm not in a cage.

The adventure life puts you face-to-face with fear, pain, hunger, and exhaustion. And until you've confronted their absence, you'll never appreciate the most ordinary things — food, water, rest, safety. It makes you realize that maybe they're not ordinary after all. Just ask any one of my students.

One of the central tenants of Buddhism is this idea that life is suffering. To an American, that might seem frightening or nihilistic. But to a monkey, its heart pounding, fleeing up a tree to escape a crocodile? I think it might tell you that suffering is the point. Only through the lens of suffering can you can see your life for what it is: a precious and fragile thing you must fight to protect.

And if your life isn't worth fighting for, what's it worth at all?

*

I started seeing the signs for 50,000 Silver Dollars, and it cheered me up.

50,000 SILVER DOLLARS, they announced. BAR * GIFT SHOP * RESTAURANT * RV PARK * CASINO * MOTEL

I'd been here before, in an 18-wheeler. Back then, I was an insecure 26-year-old on my first adventure, getting away from the Atlanta party scene and realizing there was more to life than getting drunk and sleeping with strangers. How funny that this turned out to be a place I'd visit twice. That this tacky, gimmicky truck stop would end up being a checkpoint in my life. I took a moment to reflect and reset with a root beer.

After 50,000 Silver Dollars, I opted to follow the bike path. For awhile, riding the highs of sugar and nostalgia, things were all right. And then, to my dread and dismay, the bike path dwindled and led to a road that led back to… the interstate.

I felt myself wanting to have another meltdown, so I did the most logical thing I could think of: Smoked a joint, made a playlist of all my favorite Kanye West songs, and got back on my bike. Sometimes the hardest part of doing the hard thing is accepting that you have to do it.

As soon as I got on the interstate, a green minibus slowed, the windows rolled down, and a chorus of voices from inside cheered me on. And within like seven Kanye West songs, the sign came into view:

LOOKOUT PASS:
ELEVATION 4710 FEET

I did it. I got through Montana.

There was a ski area at the summit, so I pulled into the parking lot and drank some water. I thought about this place, how I'd visited it on 18 wheels and 2, and all the places I'd been in between.

*

My introduction to Idaho involved coasting down a dirt road through a forest of tall, dignified Douglas firs. Eventually the road spit me out into a small town, where I had to stop and take a picture of the incomprehensibly beautiful sight before me.

The Trail of the Cour d'Alees. **A paved bike path.**

I wanted to get off my bike and kiss it.

I continued coasting down and down and down into Wallace — the center of the universe, according to a street sign in the middle of town.

As luck would have it, I got there the night of the annual Historic Wallace Blues Festival. It was exactly what you'd expect from a small-town blues festival in rural Idaho: white guys playing happy blues. I couldn't have been more delighted. My day ended with me sitting on a curb and enjoying live music beneath an evening sky the color of honeyed whiskey and streaked with paintwater clouds.

---

diner break: brooks restaurant (wallace, idaho)

Kinda fitting, wouldn't ya say? Brooks Restaurant is the kind of place where the regulars banter between tables and the waitress sits down to join them. There were four big guys at the table next to mine, and they asked me lots of questions and bought my breakfast. Not to be outdone, another guy walked up to my table and silently handed me a pin with a cartoon prospector and the words "Wallace, ID: The Center of the Universe." And on my way out, an elderly woman told me, "You can make it."

A day in the life: Bought a new tube to replace my patched-up, worn-out spare, and promptly got a flat a few miles later. Went to install my brand-new tube, only to find that the packaging said Presta but the valve was actually a Schrader. Unusable, in other words.

A retired judge and his retired lawyer wife tried to help me patch the flat, but my bike pump was refusing to cooperate, so they offered to just drive me to the next bike shop. I weighed my guilt at skipping 33 miles and a 2,400-foot climb against this obvious sign from the universe and accepted the ride.

At the bike shop, a short guy with an army haircut and a moisture-wicking shirt stretched taut across his pecs told me his story. He had tried to commit suicide by hiking the Appalachian Trail totally underprepared, then married a girl he'd known for four days, got arrested, got divorced, quit drugs, got really into working out, and now he's a fitness model on Instagram. The new American dream?

Eastern Washington
104 days· 4,762 miles

On a bike path in eastern Washington, I came up behind a guy on a brand-new bicycle with the cleanest, squarest panniers you've ever seen. If I had to guess, I'd say he was an engineer or an accountant with a week off, so he went to REI, bought a bunch of biking gear, and went for it. I glided up beside him and struck up a conversation, and quickly realized you can't judge a person by their panniers.

"What do you do?"

"I'm retired. I was a Marine and then I did contract work in the Middle East for 12 more years."

"Oh dope! I'm a Returned Peace Corps Volunteer and I do contract work in Antarctica!"

And thus a friendship was born.

"The Marines are, like, the hardest hardcore branch of the military, right?"

"You could say that, yeah."

"Was it scary?"

"Not really. In a combat situation, your training takes over. But before I was in the Marines, I was kind of a… reckless kid, I guess you could say. I didn't have fear. That's what drew me to it. I thought it might straighten me out."

"Did it?"

"Yes and no. The thing is, in the Marines chaos became my normal. When I got done, I couldn't handle the real world just yet, so I stayed and did contract work in Saudi, Kuwait, Iraq,

Afghanistan… and finally after 12 years my friends were like, 'Cliff, you gotta get out. You're getting squirrely.'"

"That does sound like a lot."

"Fuckin a! So I get back, and I can't function in normal situations anymore. The VA tells me I've got PTSD, and they put me on medication, but it made me crazy. I got depressed, took stupid risks, started fights… I literally stopped giving a fuck whether I lived or died."

"Wow. I'm so sorry you went through that. How did you, I mean… Do you feel like that's behind you now?"

"Oh, yeah. I found yoga two years ago, and that's what's gotten to me where I am today. That and weed."

"Dude, I *love* yoga and weed!"

It was my favorite kind of conversation: an interesting person letting me interrogate them. We immediately fell into that easy familiarity that exists between travelers. I've never been to Saudi Arabia and he's never been to Malawi. Our experiences could not have been more disparate. But beneath our differences, we share a common urge to fling ourselves off to some faraway place.

We biked together on and off all day. Classic tortoise and the hare: I was faster, but he caught me during my lengthy breaks. As much as I'd insisted on doing my tour alone, I found it was actually nice to have someone to share experiences with. Like when we passed through a literal cloud of ladybugs —

"What's up with all those ladybugs?!" I hollered back at Cliff.

"I think I inhaled a couple!"

— or when we found ourselves on an eight-mile-long road that was just loose gravel over washboard. Like riding a rumble strip. The Returned Peace Corps Volunteer and the Marine Corps veteran griped to each other about how bad they had it.

When we got to the Sprague Lake Resort, Cliff produced one of those giant headshop joints the size of a pretzel rod, and we smoked half of it sitting by the lake. I sat and stretched and listened to his wild stories about the Marines, overblown government spending, remaining calm in a war zone, and his theory that "There are two kinds of people: Heroin and meth."

The next day, I lingered too long in Jake's Cafe and didn't start making miles until after noon. The waitresses warned me that 395 was too busy for a bike, so I devised an alternate route. Mapsy made it seem perfectly plausible, but when I was actually negotiating the shadeless dirt road that climbed hill after towering hill through an unending field of wheat, I felt like an ant traversing the flames of a campfire. It was 97 degrees and all my water tasted like melted plastic and road grit.

I looked to one side and saw a buck standing regally atop a golden hill, its antlers flared like flexing biceps. Across the road, atop an adjacent golden hill, sat an 18-wheeler, just off the lot, all crimson and chrome with twin stacks jutting from the cab like horns. The two kings regarded each other with grudging respect, and then the buck bounded away.

84 miles later — that's three marathons and the better part of a 10k by the way — I met Rob at Potholes State Park as the sun was setting. He found us a nice grassy spot near a lawn sprinkler. It hummed rhythmically as we watched the sky turn the color of a lilac bud or a cold scar.

*

The Vantage Bridge was the only way I could cross the Columbia River, but I wasn't looking forward to half a mile of no shoulder and a 65 mph speed limit. I figured it would be safest to just hitch across. The first person to pull over was in an 18-wheeler, which struck me as odd, but I walked over.

The trucker asked flatly, "What is your name."

Not "Where are you going," which is the standard question someone asks when you're hitchhiking. "What is your name." Red flag. But he had an accent, and I was willing to write it off as a cross-cultural misunderstanding.

"Uh, Brooke. I just need a lift across the river, but I don't think my bike will fit in your truck."

"Where are you going."

I gave him a quick rundown of my trip, and he responded, "So you are homeless."

Two red flags. I didn't owe this guy anything, so I walked away.

He got out of his truck, and my stomach sank. I kept him in the corner of my eye as he walked around to the other side of his trailer. *Ugh, he's taking a leak.* I straddled my bike in case I needed to make a quick getaway.

He walked up to me and said, "Do you know how to do blowjob?"

"Keep walking," I spat.

He said something unintelligible, and I said firmly, "Get away from me."

He gave me a look like, "You're not worth it" and climbed back into his truck. Just then, an SUV pulled into the parking lot. Beyond the windshield, I saw a smiling couple. The timing was uncanny, like we'd planned it. The truck slithered out of the parking lot.

"Need a lift?"

"Yeah!" I said. "I'm just going across the Vantage Bridge — there's no shoulder and the speed limit is 65."

"That's good thinking," the woman said. "Well, the car's pretty full, but if we can fit your bike—"

"Oh, you're not kidding!"

The trunk was crammed with luggage, and both the backseats were down, but the guy had already gotten out and started enthusiastically rearranging things. Who was I to argue? We managed to squeeze Lucky in the back, and I crawled on top of the seats.

"Thank you so much! I'm Brooke, what are your names?"

I swear to god I'm not making this up:

"I'm Ray," he said.

"And I'm Angel."

Ellensburg, Wash.
106 days · 4,963 miles

Thomas has a heart of gold. During his summer break last year, he did an extended cross-country ride to raise money for survivors of childhood sexual abuse. These days, he's living with two other college students in a big house owned by an elderly woman.

"She's like my sweet adopted grandmother," he told me. "She lets us live here for next to nothing, so we spend time with her and help her out around the house."

We could have talked more, but he and his girlfriend were heading out on a camping trip. And so I hung out with the sweet adopted grandmother. It didn't take long before I realized she had dementia. Her stories blended together like diluted watercolors.

I left to get dinner, and when I got back Grandma was on the patio. The furniture was lovingly mismatched, all wicker and overstuffed cushions. She was sitting on a loveseat holding her dog in her lap, a skeletal wire-haired Chihuahua.

"I cut his nails," she told me, and showed me a tissue spotted with blood. The dog trembled and licked its paws.

*

I woke up just before sunrise and crept out like a thief. Grandma had left a hose running in the yard all night, the ground mushy, wasted water spilling down the driveway. I turned it off and rode into the cool, rosewater morning light, awash in confusion and guilt. I should have done something to help her. But what could I do? Was it even my place? I was so tired, and the end was so close...

I stopped perhaps a mile later at a Starbucks. There were already students hunched over their laptops and a line of people stopping for coffee on their way to work, curved like candy canes over their phones. The picture of normalcy, a song in 4/4 and the key of C. And I, an accidental.

I took my coffee outside. There are few greater pleasures than sipping hot coffee on a cool morning in a hoodie. I watched the normal people filing into Starbucks, and turned to my bike and smiled at her like we shared a wonderful secret. My girl Lucky.

GOD I LOVE THIS BIKE

I wrote in my diary.

> I really love her. Not b/c she rides well or anything. Totally average bike. But she's been the only constant. I love her personality: strong, reliable, down for anything. She's almost childlike in her enthusiasm and sense of adventure. She doesn't need much to keep running. She's beautiful in her own wild way.

I dropped my pen and smiled, because at that exact moment, I had an epiphany: A bike doesn't have a personality! A bike is just a clever arrangement of metal, plastic, and leather. All those nice things I just wrote? I was talking about *me*!

It felt like that moment after my senior prom, when I looked in a mirror after 40 days and felt like I was meeting an old friend. Underneath all the fear and doubt, even with Maple and Fiddlehead constantly squabbling, I guess I like myself after all. Beaming, I scrawled in big letters across the center of the page:

I am Lucky.

*

Tom Waits once said, "The theory is that if somebody rides a bicycle long enough, eventually the bicycle becomes 30 percent human and you become 70 percent bicycle. It's like the things that you have in your pocket. If you are carrying them there long enough, they take on certain atomic human characteristics." He also once sang that, "Anywhere, anywhere, anywhere I lay my head / I'm gonna call my home."

What if "where's home?" is the wrong question? What if home isn't a place at all, but a *relationship*?

This is hardly an original thought. The anthropologist Michael Jackson has written whole books about it, calling the sensation "being-at-home-in-the-world" — an emotional connection between body and environment. It's a connection we start learning how to make the instant we're born; after all, an infant's first experience of "place" is in its parents' arms.

That's powerful, isn't it? The first place you ever went was a hug.

Warmth, food, a heartbeat; comfort, security, love. Gradually, these concepts merge into this idea we call "home." For some people, it's one place; they're content to stay firmly fixed as coral. But we travelers drift like sea turtles tracing the earth's magnetic fields, finding our homes exactly where we are. The place, after all, isn't what's important. It's the love.

*

I wobble and veer along the bike path, eyes glued to my cell phone. Strava ticks off the miles $1/\text{10th}$ at a time until it reaches the magic number: 32.4. I come to a stop. With that, I have biked 5,000 miles.

I smile expectantly, waiting for whatever emotion happens when you ride your bike 5,000 miles. A light breeze shuffles the leaves overhead, and a few birds chirp. I clear my throat. I'm not feeling much of anything: tired mostly, kinda hungry.

Aha! I snap my fingers and smile; I've got just the thing. I lean Lucky against a tree and gather up some pine needles, twigs, and rocks. Squatting in the middle of the trail, I carefully arrange them, and then nod and stand up to admire my handiwork:

5000

I gaze at it and frown. This isn't working. On the Appalachian Trail, mile markers were a cause for celebration. What's wrong with me?

The realization begins to dawn. On the AT, we all hiked the same miles. But this 5,000 was mine alone. And unlike on the Trail, it wasn't exact. What about the times I forgot to turn on Strava and had to estimate my mileage? This could easily be mile 4,997.6, or 5,004.8. What if you counted my training rides? Then it was probably closer to 5,200, and what the hell does 5,200 mean?

I try to drum up a sense of pride or accomplishment, *something*, but all I feel is a pang of melancholy. This patch of gravel bike path, with trees on one side and a fenced-in field on the other, means nothing to anyone in the world but me.

That's okay, I think. *I bet this little spot would be pretty excited to find out it meant anything at all to anyone, let alone something really significant, even just to one person.*

That's the emotion you feel at mile 5,000, I guess: consolation. So I lean in the shade next to Lucky and take this moment to appreciate something unremarkable.

*

Around mile 5,003, I cross paths with a perfect mystery. A guy on a loaded touring bike, so he must be on a long trip… only he's wearing a plaid button-down and jeans and Keds, so maybe he's just going to work? But what commute involves a remote bike path on a Wednesday afternoon? I doubt a guy out

on a casual ride would strap a full-sized air pump to his bike…
but if he's on tour, he's traveling super-light — look how small
those panniers are!

We share a smile and come to a stop. "How far are you
going?" he asks.

"Seattle!" I say, and then add shyly, "I actually just passed
5,000 miles. You'll see my marker a little ways down the trail."

He meets my eye and says, sincerely, "Congratulations."

"Thank you. How far have you gone?"

Cocking his head and squinting up at the trees, he says,
"This is… probably… 48,000 miles."

"Are you kidding me?!"

Meet Jim. He's been touring for three years. He bikes until
he runs out of money, and then he makes his way to L.A., where
he works bike delivery gigs and sleeps on the beach. When he
has enough in the bank, he takes off again.

"I used to work in an office," he admits.

"Me too!"

"It's unfulfilling, isn't it?"

"Dude, it *sucked*!"

"I had a Toyota Camry…"

"I had a Honda Civic!"

We share a laugh.

"It's all just stuff," he says. "I used to have a whole house
full of stuff."

We grin at each other like a couple of runaway inmates. And
then he shares that today he's been "putting Pee Wee Herman
in movies where he doesn't belong. Like *Pulp Fiction*. And then
playing it out!"

And here it is: the wave of emotion I was hoping for. And
the emotion is pride. Pride that I belong to this strangest of
communities: nomadic hermits, united precisely by our rootless
solitude. Here I am, with a lonely 5,000 miles behind me, and

here is Jim, with 10 times more. Here are two solo travelers with one shared history. Here is a man who knows how to play "The Computer Dog!"

In a Pee Wee voice, he says, "A Big Mac's a Big Mac, but they call it Le Big Mac."

For a moment, my mouth hangs agape in an astonished grin, and then I throw my head back and laugh. "Jim my dude, it was a pleasure to meet you."

If you're ever in L.A., and you decide to get some food delivered — hamburgers, say — and the delivery guy is named Jim, and he has a button-down plaid shirt and permanent helmet hair, know that he's biked 50,000 miles to give you those hamburgers. And maybe, after you've tipped him 30%, you could tell him in your best Pee Wee Herman: "Hamburgers! The cornerstone of any nutritious breakfast."

*

I sprawled on a futon mattress in a ski lodge nestled in the woods at the top of a mountain and realized that I was already living in a memory. Tomorrow I would reenter the real world; tomorrow was the last day of my bike tour. It felt like I was coming out of a dream. Or maybe sinking into a different one.

It was good, for a while, to live beneath the sky, wholly at the mercy of gods, people, fate, and luck.

*

The last day of an adventure is like moving out of an apartment. Everything's packed in the moving van, and you take one last walk around this clean, empty space, marveling at how you used to fill it, how quickly you were erased.

It's these liminal moments that allow you to glimpse the transformation of the present into the past. It's here that you realize that memories are diaphanous, thin as thread. But knit together, they make up the fabric of your life.

240

So go ahead Brooke, sing your way through this last long tunnel. Sing for miles in the cold, dark, moist air, with your voice echoing off those damp stone walls. Sing all the way down the mountain if you like. Eat a pint of Ben & Jerry's under a tree in front of a Sheraton Hotel, why not? Be wild while you can. Eat blackberries from the bushes on the side of the bike path. Shake out your wrists, roll out your shoulders, rise up to give your butt a little rest, and savor the pain. It'll be gone soon, and you never know, there might come a time when you look back on that pain with a wistful little smile.

I saw a road sign that made me stop. It was a picture of a bicycle, and underneath, the words "TO SEATTLE."

That's goddam right, I thought.

I saw buildings in the distance that loomed up until I was among them. And just like that, I was another pain-in-the-ass biker clogging up traffic. Lost amidst the tangled energy of all the people on their own journeys. A grand tapestry and I a single sun-faded thread. Or maybe it was fine-spun gold.

I saw another touring cyclist and pulled up beside her and asked how far she was going. She was a kid from Australia on holiday, doing a trip from here to Arizona.

"How far are you going?" she asked.

I laughed. "Uh, I'm here. I came from the other side of the country. I've been at it for three months."

"You're finishing *today??*"

I was just as surprised as she was.

*

My finish line was nowhere special, just a city park called Myrtle Edwards. I'd arranged to meet some friends there at 3 or so, but I secretly planned to arrive an hour early. I had this picture in my head of how it would go: I'd wade out into the sound, just up to my ankles, and dip Lucky's front tire.

We did it, Lucky, I'd think.

241

I'd stand there in my sun-baked, worn-down, aching, hungry body, and I would smile and close my eyes. For a breath, I would feel the glow of triumph and pride, and I would think something profound that perfectly summed up my trip. Something about self-reliance, struggle, solitude, and love.

"Excuse me," I'd say to a stranger. "Will you take my picture?"

But when I got to Myrtle Edwards, Rob was there. Of course. He was always there. From the time I decided what to call this quixotic project, to our roadtrip to Montréal, to Potholes, to all the times I called or texted him, to all the times he'd been on my mind, to this very moment — Rob had been with me through my entire trip. I didn't let him come along on his unicycle, but like a good friend, he was still always there.

And not just him. All the people who'd helped along the way. All the people giving me their prayers and words of encouragement. All the connections I'd found and made and strengthened. Even on that beach in Illinois, in the expanse of South Dakota, in the jaws of Montana, I was surrounded by love. Could I really say I'd done this trip alone? Of course not.

"You're early!" he said.

"So are you."

He looked at me expectantly, waiting perhaps for those profound words I thought I'd have when I finally, triumphantly arrived. I looked at my friend with a smile. I searched inside myself, and coming up empty, gave a little laugh and a shrug.

"Well..." I said. "I guess that's it."

And then we sat on a rock and named all the boats in the harbor.

Seattle, Wash.
108 days · 5,084 miles

epilogue

It was like an optical illusion when I saw Friday again. When you get to know a kid, they stay a kid in your mind. Did Friday have an older brother I didn't know about? But the way he carried himself was the same. His hand still moved when he talked, still weighing something invisible and lightweight in his palm. He remained as effortlessly intelligent as I'd remembered, even more comfortable and competent and creative with English. Talking to him felt like talking to Freza, and I felt a ripple of real hope that he had what it takes to succeed at an American university.

But at our first meeting, when I arrived with a stack of admissions brochures and essay questions ready to dig into this project, he said he had to leave after 30 minutes. He assured me he'd be back tomorrow. He wasn't. Nor was he back the next day. He finally showed up three days later, and an hour later than when we'd agreed to meet. I asked what was going on, and he admitted that he'd been spending time with his girlfriend.

"She got 17 points on MSCE," he said dreamily. "She's going to university in Mzuzu."

Aha.

"Applying to American colleges is a lot of work," I said. "I won't be upset if you don't want to try."

"I want to try," he insisted.

But his actions spoke otherwise. He wrote a couple solid essays, but I never felt like I broke through his shell of distraction.

He didn't get into an American university.

We didn't get enough essays done while I was in Malawi, and it was hard to coach him from McMurdo. He missed a key meeting with the EducationUSA representative that would have qualified him for an SAT fee waiver. His head just wasn't in the game.

I maintain that Friday is one of the most gifted people I've ever met. And I acknowledge that he totally screwed up a good opportunity. In the end, you can't make other people do what you want them to do, even if you only want the best for them. You can be disappointed or frustrated, I guess, but I feel like it's better to be happy for them, because they're learning. I bet he and 18-year-old Brooke would have been friends.

But it's not like Represent the Village was a total bust. Samuel and Davie got into Machinga Teacher Training College, and the tuition was so affordable that I was able to cover all two years of their education, plus helping out with tuition and fees for eight other needy students. Cameron ended up not going back to school, but Charles was accepted to Bunda College, one of the best schools in Malawi. The money we raised was enough to pay for his first year, and he ended up finding a scholarship for the remaining three years. Maybe everything worked out the way it was supposed to.

Life in the village had gone on, and my students had grown up. Of course I understood this before I came back, but not quite how it would manifest. Aubrey got married, and his first child was on the way. Yusuf was married too. They had both been star students, and they both ended up as farmers. They both seemed happy.

I stayed with Madam Phiri. We'd watch the terrible movies America exports to Africa and chat. Not being a representative of the Peace Corps made it easier to stray from cultural norms, so we talked about drinking and sex.

"Soldiers' wives must take wine," she laughed. "We would drink just too much. Some could sleep! Others could uri*nate*!"

She's estranged from her husband. He sounds like a dog; he has a new wife, and Madam Phiri is raising his kids all by herself — in addition to supporting her extended family. I asked if she'd ever remarry, and she gave me a look that said, "Girl, can't you see that a husband is essentially another child you have to take care of?"

"What about sex?" I asked.

"I do not have that appetite," she said. She considered the matter for a moment, and then added, "No. NO. NOOOOOOOO!"

*

It just so happened that the new Peace Corps Volunteer was moving in, and the gal who'd succeeded me came back to visit. And so three generations of PCVs climbed Ngusa, the hill behind the school, and looked out over the village of Chikweo. I gazed at it with fuzzy nostalgia. Nyassa, who'd been living in Malawi for three years, regarded it with the levelheaded clarity of a seasoned expat. Maddie looked at it with starry-eyed optimism, with anticipation and maybe a touch of apprehension, as something large and unfamiliar first coming into view.

Funny how the same place can have three different meanings to three different people. Funny how all those meanings are home.

The day I left, I boarded a minibus and gazed out the window at the tan landscape dotted with oregano-colored scrub brush. At the end of my time as a PCV, a minibus ride was a tedious chore to be endured. But now I was soaking up every moment. Like I had died and come back to life, and now I was savoring every mosquito bite.

*

Is it hard to ride your bike across the country?

Yep. Scary too.

But just because something's hard and scary doesn't mean you shouldn't do it. In fact, I think it means you should. What if your weakness is just the strength you have to earn? What if your fear is a deeply buried dream — like a seed beneath a sidewalk?

What's a seed for anyway, if not to grow?

THE END

acknowledgements

Rob, I love you dearly. Your friendship is a gift.

Friday, Samuel, Davie, Cameron, Charles, Gladys, Linly, Leticia, Sifati, Cidrick, Freza, and Tawonga: Thank you for being a constant source of inspiration for me. I'm so proud of all of you, and I know you're going to do great things in your lives.

Evan, this book wouldn't have happened without your generosity... mwahahaha, that's right, now everyone knows you're secretly nice!

Chelsea, Zummi, and Abi at Diner @ Manayunk: Thank you for all the refills and words of encouragement.

Marco, you played a much bigger role in this trip than I portrayed in this book. Thank you for being there for me when I needed someone to talk to. I'm sorry for the imbalance in our friendship, and I wish you nothing but the best.

Megan, you're the definition of a good friend. Thank you and Neal for giving me a nice place to stay and not making a big fuss about me.

Mom, you and your friends are the best role models a gal could ask for. Thanks for your limitless support, and for giving me a place to stay between adventures.

Dad, I love you and admire you so much and brag about you to all my friends. Thank you for teaching me how to be tough.

Jill, thank you for forever pushing me to be the best version of myself.

Christina and Nikki, thanks for writing with me.

To everyone I met on my tour who offered me words of encouragement, who smiled at me, who opened up their homes to me: I'm sorry I couldn't share all these stories, but believe me, your kindness is eternally appreciated. You proved to me that the world is not nearly as scary as everyone says it is, and I have tried to pay it forward at every opportunity. Special thanks go out to Abbie and Jared, Neil, Jim and Wendy, Gerald and Susan, Melissa, Cat, Meghan, Ihab, Robyn, Nancy, Olive Oil, Stephanie, Gina and Patrick, Peter and Debra, Ucrious, Brandon and Lulu, Robert, Danielle, Anne and Chatterbox, Jake and his housemates, Jim and Jennifer, Mark and Celeste, Mike and Alyson, Andy, Heidi and Ernie, Rona and Jack, Myriad and Dan, Evan, Edwin and Janice, Aunt Skeet, Amos and Jeanie, Thorny, Jane and Pete, Aunt Claire, Ellen and Bill, Dad, Whisper, Jill, Wayne, Todd, Nancy and Ken, Shaun and Wes, Dafna, Adrian and Diana, Malcolm, Jen, Barb and Brian, Suzette, Alice and Philip, Andy, Laura, Jake, Pete and Marolyn, Geoff and Pat, Kelly, David H., John and LeAnn, Jeremy and his housemates, Donna and Adam, Franz and Catherine, Terry, Melinda, David F., Marco, and Meg and Neal.

To everyone who donated to Represent the Village: You made a personal sacrifice for those less fortunate, and your actions had a measurable positive impact on 12 people's lives. You should be so proud of yourselves. Thank you.

And Doug –you marvelous human– thank you for making a place in your heart and your home for Lucky and me.

sources

"Dream." *Online Etymology Dictionary.*
http://www.etymonline.com/word/dream. Accessed 9 July 2019.

Koerner, Konrad. "The Sapir-Whorf Hypothesis: A Preliminary History and a Bibliographical Essay." *Journal of Linguistic Anthropology,* vol. 2, no. 2, December 1992, pp. 173-198.

Medina, Jennifer, Benner, Katie, and Taylor, Kate. "Actresses, Business Leaders and Other Wealthy Parents Charged in U.S. College Entry Fraud." *New York Times,* 12 March 2019.

@mrtrashwheel. *Facebook.* www.facebook.com/mrtrashwheel. Accessed 11 March 2021.

Albanese, Catherine L. "Exploring Regional Religion: A Case Study of the Eastern Cherokee." *History of Religions,* vol. 23, no. 4, May 1984, pp. 344-371.

Whitman, Walt. "Song of Myself." *Leaves of Grass.* 1892 "Deathbed" edition.

The Community College of Philadelphia. www.ccp.edu. Accessed 14 March 2020.

"About Us." *College Board,* about.collegeboard.org. Accessed 23 February 2020.

Schenck, Laura. "Small Family Farms Country Factsheet: Malawi." *Food and Agriculture Organization of the United Nations,* 2018.

"Crime in Philadelphia: Hunting Park." *Philly.com.* data.philly.com/philly/crime/?dNeigh=Hunting%20Park&nType=crime. Accessed 15 November 2020.

International Atomic Energy Agency. "Ten Years After Chernobyl: What Do We Really Know?" *IAEA/WHO/EC International Conference,* Vol. 28, No. 13, 1996, pp. 8.

The Babushkas of Chernobyl. Directed by Holly Morris and Anne Bogart, performances by Hanna Zavorotyna, Maria Shovkuta, and Valentyna Ivanivna, Chicken and Egg Pictures, 2015.

Miranda, Lin-Manuel. "Alexander Hamilton," Atlantic Records, 2015.

Making Caring Common Project. *Turning the Tide: Inspiring Concern for Others and the Common Good Through College Admissions*. Cambridge: Harvard Graduate School of Education, 2016.

Waits, Tom. *Tom Waits on Tom Waits: Interviews and Encounters*, edited by Paul Maher. Chicago, Chicago Review Press, 20.

Nietzel, Michael T. "College Enrollment Declines Again. It's Down More Than Two Million Students In This Decade." *Forbes*, 16 December 2019.

National Center for Education Statistics. "Price of Attending an Undergraduate Institution." nces.ed.gov/programs/coe/indicator_cua.asp. Accessed 11 February 2020.

Mitchell, Michael, Leachman, Michael, and Masterson, Kathleen. "A Lost Decade in Higher Education Funding: State Cuts Have Driven Up Tuition and Reduced Quality." *Center on Budget and Policy Priorities.* www.cbpp.org/research/state-budget-and-tax/a-lost-decade-in-higher-education-funding. Accessed 11 February 2020.

Issa, Natalie. "U.S. Average Student Loan Debt Statistics in 2019." *Credit.com.* www.credit.com/personal-finance/average-student-loan-debt. Accessed 11 February 2020.

Mitchell, Michael, Leachman, Michael, and Masterson, Kathleen. "Funding Down, Tuition Up: State Cuts to Higher Education Threaten Quality and Affordability at Public Colleges." *Center on Budget and Policy Priorities* www.cbpp.org/research/state-budget-and-tax/funding-down-tuition-up. Accessed 11 February 2020.

National Center for Education Statistics. "Fast Facts: Expenditures." nces.ed.gov/fastfacts/display.asp?id=75. Accessed 11 February 2020.

Greenwald, Richard A. "Protecting Tenure." *Inside Higher Ed.* www.insidehighered.com/views/2019/03/14/overlooked-administrative-and-financial-benefits-tenure-opinion. Accessed 11 February 2020.

Flaherty, Colleen. "A Non Tenure-Track Profession?" *Inside Higher Ed.* www.insidehighered.com/news/2018/10/12/about-three-quarters-all-faculty-positions-are-tenure-track-according-new-aaup. Accessed 11 February 2020.

Kingkade, Tyler. "9 Reasons Why Being an Adjunct Faculty Member is Terrible." *HuffPost.* www.huffpost.com/entry/adjunct-faculty_n_4255139. Accessed 11 February 2020.

Ginsberg, Benjamin. "Administrators Ate My Tuition." *Washington Monthly*. washingtonmonthly.com/magazine/septoct-2011/administrators-ate-my-tuition. Accessed 11 February 2020.

Salary.com. "College President Salary in the United States." www.salary.com/research/salary/benchmark/college-president-salary. Accessed 11 February 2020.

Thoreau, Henry David. *Walden*. London: J.M. Dent, 1908.

Niagara Falls State Park. "Facts About Niagara Falls." www.niagarafallsstatepark.com/niagara-falls-state-park/amazing-niagara-facts. Accessed 29 July 2019.

Clark, Alexis. "After the Underground Railroad, Harriet Tubman Led a Brazen Civil War Raid." *History*. www.history.com/news/harriet-tubman-combahee-ferry-raid-civil-war. Accessed 8 August 2019.

Oberlin College and Conservatory. "Oberlin History." www.oberlin.edu/about-oberlin/oberlin-history. Accessed 24 January 2020.

Lao Tzu. *Tao Te Ching*. New York: Vintage Books, 1972.

The Heidelberg Project. "History." www.heidelberg.org/history. Accessed 13 July 2019.

National Park Service. "1933 Chicago World's Fair Century of Progress Homes." www.nps.gov/indu/learn/historyculture/centuryofprogress.htm. Accessed 19 July 2019.

Eberhardt, Isabelle. *The Nomad*. Northhampton, Interlink Books, 2003.

Vossler, Bill. "North Dakota's Enchanted Highway." *The Saturday Evening Post*. 17 December 2008.

Melroy, Mark. *Islands on the Prairie: The Mountain Ranges of Eastern Montana*. Farcountry Press, Helena, 1986.

"Scientific Opinion on Animal health and welfare risks associated with the import of wild birds other than poultry into the European Union." *The EFSA Journal* No. 410, 2006, 1-55.

Horton M., Wright N., Dyer W., et al. "Assessing the risk of self-harm in an adult offender population: an incidence cohort study." *Health Technology Assessment*, Vol. 18, No. 64, 2014.

de Jonghe-Rouleau, Adrienne P., Pot, Anne Margriet, de Jonghe, Jos F. M. "Self-Injurious Behaviour in nursing home residents with dementia." *International Journal of Geriatric Psychiatry*, Vol. 20, No. 7, 2005, pp. 651-657.

Repp, Alan C., Felce, David, and Barton, Lyle E. "Basing the Treatment of Sterotypic and Self-Injurious Behaviors on Hypotheses of Their Causes." *Journal of Applied Behavioral Analysis*, Vol. 21, No. 3, 1988, pp. 281-289.

Statesman Staff. "Wallace, Idaho Declared 'Center of the Universe.'" *Idaho Statesman*, 14 July 2016.

Pulp Fiction. Directed by Quentin Tarantino, performances by John Travolta, Uma Thurman, and Samuel L. Jackson, Miramax, 1994.

Waits, Tom. "Anywhere I Lay My Head," Island Records, 1985.

Jackson, Michael. At Home in the World. Durham, Duke University Press Books, 2000.

about the author

Brooke Marshall is a writer, educational advocate, traveler, and visual artist who has helped 12 Malawian students pursue their education. She is currently in the process of establishing The Represent Foundation, a nonprofit that will allow her to continue to advocate for needy students. She lives with her partner in a 2018 Ford Transit.

www.representfoundation.org
www.slimrims.com

Made in the USA
Columbia, SC
28 November 2021